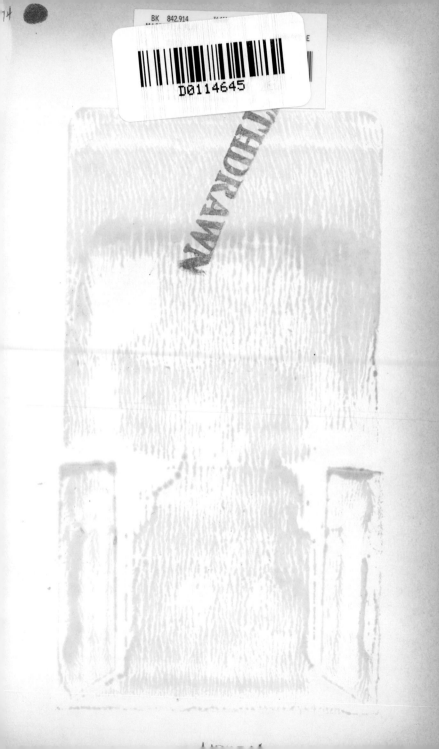

MACBETT

OTHER WORKS BY EUGÈNE IONESCO

PUBLISHED BY GROVE PRESS

MACBETT

A PLAY BY
EUGÈNE IONESCO

Translated from the French
by Charles Marowitz

GROVE PRESS, INC.
NEW YORK

ISBN: 0-394-17805-X

Library of Congress Catalog Number: 73-6644

FIRST EVERGREEN EDITION

First Printing

Manufactured in the United States of America by American Book–Stratford Press, New York

PERFORMANCE NOTICE

Macbett was first performed on January 27, 1972 at the Théâtre de la Rive Gauche in Paris.

The English language premiere was performed by the Yale Repertory Theatre in New Haven, Connecticut on March 16, 1973. It was directed by William Peters, John McAndrew and Alvin Epstein; music composed by Gregory Sandow; sound by Carol M. Waaser; scenery design by Enno Poersch; lighting design by Ian Rodney Calderon; costume design by Maura Beth Smolover; and with the following cast:

MACBETT	Alvin Epstein
DUNCAN	Eugene Troobnick
LADY DUNCAN	
LADY MACBETT	Carmen de Lavallade
FIRST WITCH	
SECOND WITCH	
LADY IN WAITING	Deborah Mayo
MAID	Amandina Lihamba
GLAMISS	John McAndrew
CANDOR	William Peters
BANCO	
MONK	Stephen Joyce
MACOL	
BISHOP	Michael Gross

PERFORMANCE NOTICE

SOLDIERS, GENERALS,
BUTTERFLY HUNTER,
GUESTS, CROWD,
LEMONADE SELLER,
ETC.
}
Josepha G. Grifasi
Michael Gross
Amandina Lihamba
John McCaffrey
Paul Schierhorn
Michael Quigley

MACBETT

A field.

GLAMISS *and* CANDOR. GLAMISS *enters from left as*
CANDOR *enters from right.*

*They come on without acknowledging each other
and stand center stage, facing the audience.*

Pause.

GLAMISS (*turning toward* CANDOR) Good morning,
Baron Candor.
CANDOR (*turning toward* GLAMISS) Good morning,
Baron Glamiss.
GLAMISS Listen, Candor.
CANDOR Listen, Glamiss.
GLAMISS This can't go on.
CANDOR This can't go on.

GLAMISS *and* CANDOR *are angry. Their anger and
derision become more and more emphatic. One
can hardly make out what they're saying. The text
serves only as a basis for their mounting anger.*

3

GLAMISS (*derisively*)   Our sovereign . . .

CANDOR (*ditto*)   Duncan. The beloved Archduke Duncan.

GLAMISS   Yes, beloved. Well beloved.

CANDOR   Too well beloved.

GLAMISS   Down with Duncan.

CANDOR   Down with Duncan.

GLAMISS   He hunts on my land.

CANDOR   For the benefit of the State.

GLAMISS   So he says . . .

CANDOR   He *is* the State.

GLAMISS   I give him ten thousand chickens a year and their eggs.

CANDOR   So do I.

GLAMISS   It may be all right for others . . .

CANDOR   But not for me!

GLAMISS   Me neither.

CANDOR   If they're prepared to take it, that's their business . . .

GLAMISS   He's drafting my men into his army.

CANDOR   The National army.

GLAMISS   Sucking me dry.

CANDOR   Sucking us dry.

GLAMISS   Taking my men. My army. Turning my own men against me.

CANDOR   And me.

GLAMISS   Never seen anything like it.

CANDOR   My ancestors would turn over in their grave . . .

GLAMISS   So would mine!

CANDOR   And there's all his cronies and parasites.

GLAMISS   Who fat themselves on the sweat of our brow.

CANDOR   The fat of our chickens.

GLAMISS   Of our sheep.

CANDOR   Of our pigs.

GLAMISS   Swine.

CANDOR   Of our bread.

GLAMISS   Ten thousand chickens, ten thousand horses, ten thousand recruits. What does he do with them? He can't eat them all. The rest just goes bad.

CANDOR   And a thousand young girls.

GLAMISS   We know what he does with them.

CANDOR   Why should we owe him? It's he who owes us.

GLAMISS   More than he can pay.

CANDOR   Not to mention the rest.

GLAMISS   Down with Duncan.

CANDOR   Down with Duncan.

GLAMISS   He's no better than we are.

CANDOR   Worse, if anything.

GLAMISS   Much worse.

CANDOR   Much much worse.

GLAMISS   Just thinking about it makes my blood boil.

CANDOR   It really gets me worked up.

GLAMISS   My honor.

CANDOR   My glory.

GLAMISS   Our ancestral rights.

CANDOR   My property.

GLAMISS   My land.

CANDOR   Our right to happiness.

GLAMISS   He doesn't give two hoots.

CANDOR   He doesn't give one!

GLAMISS   We're not nobodies.

CANDOR   Far from it.

GLAMISS   We stand for something.

CANDOR   We're not just "things."

GLAMISS   We're nobody's fool—least of all Duncan's. Ha, beloved sovereign!

CANDOR   He won't lead me up the garden path or sell me down the river.

GLAMISS   Sell me up the river or lead me down the garden path.

CANDOR   Even in my dreams.

GLAMISS   Even in my dreams he haunts me like a living nightmare.

CANDOR   We must get rid of him.

GLAMISS   We must get rid of him—lock, stock, and barrel.

CANDOR   Lock, stock, and barrel.

GLAMISS   We want freedom.

CANDOR   The right to make more and more money. Self-rule!

GLAMISS   Liberty.

CANDOR   Running our own affairs!

GLAMISS   And his!

CANDOR   *And* his!

GLAMISS   We'll split it between us.

CANDOR   Half and half.

GLAMISS   Half and half.

CANDOR   He's a lousy administrator.

GLAMISS   He's unfair!

CANDOR   We'll establish justice.

GLAMISS   We'll reign in his stead.

CANDOR   We'll take his place.

CANDOR *and* GLAMISS *walk toward each other. They look stage right, where* BANCO *enters.*

CANDOR   Hail Banco, gallant general.

GLAMISS   Hail Banco, great captain.

BANCO   Hail Glamiss. Hail Candor.

GLAMISS (*aside to* CANDOR)   Not a word about you-know-what. He's loyal to Duncan.

CANDOR (*to* BANCO)   We were just going for a little stroll.

GLAMISS (*to* BANCO)   Very warm for this time of year.

CANDOR (*to* BANCO)   Would you like to sit down for a moment?

BANCO   No thanks. I'm taking my morning constitutional.

GLAMISS   Ah yes. Very good for your health.

CANDOR   We admire your courage, you know.

BANCO   I do my best for King and Country.

GLAMISS (*to* BANCO)   Quite right, too.

CANDOR   You're doing a grand job.

BANCO   Now gentlemen, if you'll excuse me. (*He goes out left.*)

CANDOR   Farewell, Banco.

GLAMISS   Farewell, Banco. (*To* CANDOR) We can't count on him.

CANDOR (*half drawing his sword*)   He's got his back turned. We could kill him now if you like. (*He tiptoes several paces toward* BANCO.)

GLAMISS   Not yet. The time isn't ripe. Our army is unprepared. We need more time. It will be soon enough.

CANDOR *sheathes his sword.* MACBETT *enters stage right.*

CANDOR (*to* GLAMISS)   Here's another of the Grand Duke's loyal subjects.

GLAMISS Hail Macbett.

CANDOR Hail Macbett, faithful and virtuous gentleman.

MACBETT Hail Baron Candor. Hail Baron Glamiss.

GLAMISS Hail Macbett, great general. (*Aside to* CANDOR) He mustn't suspect anything. Act natural.

CANDOR Glamiss and I are great admirers of your fidelity, your loyalty toward our beloved sovereign, the Archduke Duncan.

MACBETT Why shouldn't I be faithful and loyal? After all, I took the oath of allegiance.

GLAMISS No, that's not what we meant. On the contrary, you're quite right. Congratulations.

CANDOR His gratitude no doubt is very satisfying.

MACBETT (*with a broad smile*) The generosity of King Duncan is legendary. He always has the good of the people at heart.

GLAMISS (*winking at* CANDOR) Quite right, too.

CANDOR We're sure he does.

MACBETT Duncan is generosity incarnate. He gives away all he possesses.

GLAMISS (*to* MACBETT) You must have done quite well by him.

MACBETT He's also brave.

CANDOR Great exploits testify to his courage.

GLAMISS It's common knowledge.

MACBETT He's everything they say he is. Our sovereign is good, he's loyal, and his wife, our queen, the Archduchess, is every bit as good as she is beautiful. She is charitable. She helps the poor. She tends the sick.

CANDOR How could we not admire such a man?—A perfect man. A perfect ruler.

GLAMISS   How could we not be loyal in the face of such loyalty? How could we not be generous amidst such generosity?

MACBETT (*almost suiting the action to the word*)   I'd fight to the death against anyone who said the contrary.

CANDOR   We're convinced, absolutely convinced, that Duncan is the most virtuous ruler the world has ever known.

GLAMISS   He is virtue itself.

MACBETT   I do my best to follow his example. I try to be as courageous, virtuous, loyal, and good as he is.

GLAMISS   That's not easy.

CANDOR   Because he's a very good man indeed.

GLAMISS   And Lady Duncan is very beautiful.

MACBETT   I do my best to resemble him. Farewell, gentlemen. (*He goes off left.*)

GLAMISS   He almost convinced me, for a minute.

CANDOR   He's a believer. A . . . .

GLAMISS   He's incorruptible.

CANDOR   A dangerous character. He and Banco are the commanders-in-chief of the Archduke's army.

GLAMISS   You're not trying to back out, are you?

CANDOR   No—certainly not. I don't think so.

GLAMISS (*hand on his sword*)   Just don't try it, that's all.

CANDOR   No, I won't. I really won't. Yes, yes, of course you can count on me. Of course, of course! Of course!

GLAMISS   Right. Let's get a move on then—polish our weapons, gather our men, prepare our armies. We shall attack at dawn. Tomorrow evening Duncan will be beaten and we shall share the throne.

CANDOR   You do believe Duncan's a tyrant, don't you?

GLAMISS A tyrant, a usurper, a despot, a dictator, a miscreant, an ogre, an ass, a goose—and worse. The proof is, he's in power. If I didn't believe it, why should I want to depose him? My motives are thoroughly honorable.

CANDOR I suppose you're right.

GLAMISS Let's swear to trust each other completely.

CANDOR *and* GLAMISS *draw their swords and salute each other.*

GLAMISS I trust you and I swear on my sword to be absolutely loyal.

CANDOR I trust you and I swear on my sword to be absolutely loyal.

They sheathe their swords and go out quickly, GLAMISS *to the left,* CANDOR *to the right.*

Pause. The stage is empty. Great play should be made here with the lighting on the cyclorama and with sound effects, which eventually becomes a sort of musique concrète.

Shots are fired. Flashes. We should see the ripple of gunfire. A conflagration in the sky on the backcloth.

Equally a very bright light could come from above which would be reflected off the stage. Storm and lightning.

The sky clears. A beautiful red sky on the backcloth. A tragic sky. At the same time as the horizon clears, and turns red, the sounds of machine-gun fire become more and more infrequent and fade into the distance.

Shouts, death rattles, the groans of the wounded are heard—then more shots. A wounded man screams shrilly.

The clouds clear. A large deserted plain. The wounded man stops screaming. After two or three seconds' silence a woman's shrill scream is heard.

This should go on for a long time before the characters in the next scene appear. The lighting and the sound effects should have nothing naturalistic about them— especially toward the end. The contributions of the lighting designer and sound technicians are of crucial importance here.

Toward the end of the sound track, a SOLDIER *fences his way across the stage from left to right—flourishes, lunges, salutes, corps a corps, feints, direct attacks, all sorts of parries.* All this happens quickly.

The noises stop for a while before beginning again. Silence. The flourishes, etc., happen quickly. There should be nothing balletic about them.

A woman, disheveled and weeping, runs across the stage from left to right.

The LEMONADE SELLER *enters stage right.*

LEMONADE SELLER   Lemonade. Cool and refreshing. Soldiers and civilians, buy my lovely lemonade. Roll up, roll up. Who wants to wet his whistle? There's a truce on. Better make the most of it. Lemonade, lemonade. Cure the wounded, lemonade to keep you from getting frightened. Lemonade for soldiers. One franc a bottle, four for three francs. It's also good for scratches, cuts, and bruises.

TWO SOLDIERS *come on from left. One is carrying the other on his back.*

LEMONADE SELLER (*to the* FIRST SOLDIER)   Wounded?
SOLDIER   No. Dead.
LEMONADE SELLER   Sword?
SOLDIER   No.
LEMONADE SELLER   Bayonet?
SOLDIER   No.
LEMONADE SELLER   Pistol shot?
SOLDIER   Heart attack.

The TWO SOLDIERS *go out right.*

LEMONADE SELLER   Lemonade. Cool and refreshing. Lemonade, for soldiers. Good for the heart. Good for the shakes. The willies. The heebeejeebees.

ANOTHER SOLDIER *enters right.*

LEMONADE SELLER   Refreshing drinks.
SECOND SOLDIER   What are you selling?
LEMONADE SELLER   Lemonade. It heals wounds.
SECOND SOLDIER   I'm not wounded.
LEMONADE SELLER   Keeps you from getting scared.
SECOND SOLDIER   I'm never scared.
LEMONADE SELLER   One franc a bottle. It's good for the heart as well.
SECOND SOLDIER (*tapping his breastplate*)   I've got seven under here.
LEMONADE SELLER   Good for scratches, too.

SECOND SOLDIER   Scratches? I've certainly got a few of those. We fought long and hard. With this. (*He shows his club.*) And this. (*He shows his sword.*) But especially with this. (*He shows his dagger.*) You shove it in his belly . . . in his guts. That's the part I like best. Look, there's still some blood on it. I use it to cut my bread and cheese with.

LEMONADE SELLER   I can see well enough from here.

SECOND SOLDIER   Scared, are you?

LEMONADE SELLER (*terrified*)   Lemonade, lemonade. Good for stiff necks, colds, gout, measles, smallpox.

SECOND SOLDIER   I killed as many of 'em as I could. Mashed 'em up something horrible. They yelled and the blood spurted. What a do! It ain't always as larky as that. Give me a drink.

LEMONADE SELLER   It's on the house, general.

SECOND SOLDIER   I'm not a general.

LEMONADE SELLER   Major.

SECOND SOLDIER   I'm not a major.

LEMONADE SELLER   You soon will be, though. (*Gives him a drink.*)

SECOND SOLDIER (*after several gulps*)   Revolting. Cat's piss. What a nerve. It's daylight robbery.

LEMONADE SELLER   You can have your money back.

SECOND SOLDIER   You're shaking. You're scared. It doesn't stop you getting the shakes, does it? (*He draws his dagger.*)

LEMONADE SELLER   Don't do that—please.

A bugle call.

SECOND SOLDIER (*sheathing his dagger and going off left*)   Lucky for you I haven't got time. But just you wait. I'll get to you again.

LEMONADE SELLER (*alone, trembling*) Whew, he really scared me. I hope the other side wins and cuts him up into little pieces—minced meat and mashed potatoes. Bastard. Swine. Shithead. (*Change.*) Lemonade, lemonade. Cool and refreshing. Three francs for four.

He goes out right slowly at first, then gradually getting quicker as the SOLDIER, *with his sword and dagger, reappears stage left.*

> *The* SOLDIER *catches the* LEMONADE SELLER *just as he's going off into the wings. All we can see, in profile or from behind, is that the* SOLDIER *strikes the* LEMONADE SELLER, *and we hear him cry out. The* SOLDIER *disappears as well.*

> *The noise of shooting, screams, etc. begins again, but softer now, further away. The sky flares up again, etc.*

> MACBETT *enters upstage. He is exhausted. He sits down on a milestone. In his hand is a naked sword. He looks at it.*

MACBETT   The blade of my sword is all red with blood. I've killed dozens and dozens of them with my bare hands. Twelve dozen officers and men who never did me any harm. I've had hundreds and hundreds of others executed by firing squad. Thousands of others were roasted alive when I set fire to the forests where they'd run for safety. Tens of thousands of men, women, and children suffocated to death in cellars, buried under the rubble of their houses which I'd blown up. Hundreds of thousands were drowned in the Channel in desperate attempts to escape. Millions died of fear or committed suicide. Ten million others died of anger, apoplexy, or a broken heart. There's not enough ground to bury them all. The bloated bodies of the dead have sucked up all the water from the lakes in which they throw themselves. There's no more water. Not even enough vultures to do the job. There are still some survivors, can you imagine? They're still fighting. We must make an end of it. If you cut their heads off, the blood spurts from their throats in fountains. Gallons of blood. My soldiers drown in it. Battalions, brigades, divisions, army corps with their commanders, brigadiers first, then in descending order of rank, lieutenant-generals, major-generals and field marshals. The severed heads of our enemies spit in our face and mock us. Arms shorn from their trunks go on brandishing their swords and firing pistols. Amputated feet kick us up the backside. They were all traitors, of course. Enemies of the people—and of our beloved sovereign, the Archduke Duncan, whom God preserve. They wanted to overthrow him. With the help of foreign soldiers. I was right, I think. In the heat of battle, you often lay about you indiscriminately. I hope I didn't kill any of our friends by mistake. We were fighting shoulder to shoulder. I hope I didn't tread on their toes. Yes, we're in the right. I've come to rest awhile on this stone. I'm feeling a little queasy. I've left Banco in sole command of the army. I'll go and relieve him in a bit. It's strange—in spite of all this exertion, I haven't got much of an appetite. (*He pulls a large handkerchief out of his pocket and mops his brow and the rest of his face.*) I thrashed about a bit too hard. My wrist aches. Luckily it's nothing serious. It's been quite a pleasant day, really. Feeling quite bucked. (*He shouts to his orderly, stage right.*) Go and clean my sword in the river and bring me something to drink.

The ORDERLY *enters and goes out with the sword. He comes back immediately, without having completely left the stage.*

ORDERLY   One clean sword and a jug of wine.

MACBETT *takes the sword.*

MACBETT   Good as new.

He sheathes the sword and drinks from the jug of wine, while the ORDERLY *goes out left.*

No. No regrets. They were traitors after all. I obeyed my sovereign's orders. I did my duty. (*Putting the jug down.*) It's good, this wine. I'm quite rested now. Well, back to the grind. (*He looks upstage.*) Here's Banco. Hey. How's it going?

BANCO *or his* VOICE   They're just about retreating. Take over from me, will you? I'm going to take a bit of a breather. I'll join you in a bit.

MACBETT   We mustn't let Glamiss escape. I'll go and surround them. Quickly.

MACBETT *goes off upstage.* MACBETT *and* BANCO *resemble each other. Same costume, same beard.*

BANCO *enters right. He is exhausted. He sits down on a boundary stone. In his hand is a naked sword. He looks at it.*

BANCO   The blade of my sword is all red with blood.
I've killed dozens and dozens of them with my own
hand. Twelve dozen officers and men who never did
me any harm. I've had hundreds and hundreds of
others executed by the firing squad. Thousands of
others were roasted alive when I set fire to the forests
where they'd run for safety. Tens of thousands of
men, women and children suffocated to death in cellars, buried under the rubble of their houses which
I'd blown up. Hundreds of thousands were drowned
in the Channel in desperate attempts to escape. Millions died of fear or committed suicide. Ten million
others died of anger, apoplexy or a broken heart.
There's not enough ground to bury them all. The
bloated bodies of the dead have sucked up all the
water from the lakes in which they threw themselves.
There's no more water. Not even enough vultures to
do the job. There are still some survivors, can you
imagine? They're still fighting. We must make an
end of it. If you cut their heads off, the blood spurts
from their throats in fountains. Gallons of blood. My
soldiers drown in it. Battalions, brigades, divisions,
army corps with their commanders, brigadiers first,
then in descending order of rank, lieutenant-generals, major-generals and field marshals. The severed heads of our enemies spit in our face and
mock us. Arms shorn from their trunks go on waving
swords or firing pistols. Amputated feet kick us up
the backside. They were traitors, of course. Enemies
of the people—and of our beloved sovereign, the
Archduke Duncan, whom God preserve. They wanted
to overthrow him. With the help of foreign soldiers.
I was right, I think. In the heat of battle, you often

lay about you indiscriminately. I hope I didn't kill any of our friends by mistake. We were fighting shoulder to shoulder. I hope I didn't tread on their toes. Yes, we're in the right. I've come to rest awhile on this stone. I'm feeling a little queasy. I've left Macbett in sole command of the army. I'll go and relieve him in a bit. It's strange—in spite of all this exertion I haven't got much of an appetite. (*He pulls a large handkerchief out of his pocket and mops his brow and the rest of his face.*) I thrashed about a bit too hard. My wrist aches. Luckily it's nothing serious. It's been quite a pleasant day, really. Feeling quite bucked. (*He shouts to his orderly, stage right.*) Go and clean my sword in the river and bring me something to drink.

The ORDERLY *enters and goes out with the sword. He comes back immediately, without having completely left the stage.*

ORDERLY   One clean sword and a jug of wine.

BANCO *takes the sword.*

BANCO   Good as new.

He sheathes the sword and drinks from the jug of wine, while the ORDERLY *goes out left.*

No. No regrets. They were traitors after all. I obeyed my sovereign's orders. I did my duty. (*Putting the jug down.*) It's good, this wine. I'm quite rested now. Well, back to the grind. (*He looks upstage.*) Here's Macbett. Hey. How's it going?

MACBETT *or his* VOICE   They're just about retreating. Come and join me and we'll finish them off.

BANCO   We mustn't let Glamiss escape. We'll surround them. I'll be right with you. (BANCO *goes out upstage.*)

The sounds of battle well up again. The conflagration in the sky is brighter now.

Pounding brutal music.

A woman crosses the stage from left to right. She is quite unconcerned and has a basket over her arm as if she were going shopping.

The sound dies away again until it is little more than a background murmur.

The stage is empty for a few moments, then ridiculously lavish fanfares drown out the noise of battle.

An OFFICER *in Duncan's army comes on quickly from the left and stops stage center. He is carrying a sort of armchair or portable throne.*

OFFICER   Our lord, the Archduke Duncan and the Archduchess.

> LADY DUNCAN *and the* ARCHDUKE *come on left.* LADY DUNCAN *is in front of the* ARCHDUKE. *She is wearing a crown and a long green dress with a flower on it. She is the only character in the play who dresses with a certain flair.* DUNCAN *mounts the throne. The two others stand on either side of him.*

OFFICER Come on, my lord. It's all right. The battle has moved on. We're out of range here. Not even a sniper about. Don't be afraid. There are even people strolling about.

DUNCAN Has Candor been defeated. If so, have they executed him? Have they killed Glamiss as I ordered?

OFFICER I hope so. You should have looked a bit more closely. The horizon is all red. It looks as if they're still at it, but a long way off now. We must wait till it's over. Be patient, my lord.

DUNCAN What if Macbett and Banco have been routed?

LADY DUNCAN You take the field yourself.

DUNCAN If they've been beaten, where can I hide? The king of Malta is my enemy. So is the emperor of Cuba. *And* the prince of the Balearic Isles. And the kings of France and Ireland, and what's more, I've got lots of enemies at the English court. Where can I hide?

OFFICER It's all right, my lord. You just leave it to Macbett and Banco. They're good generals—brave, energetic, skilled strategists. They've proved their worth time and again.

DUNCAN I don't seem to have much choice. In any case I'm going to take one or two precautions. Saddle my best horse, the one who doesn't kick, and get my launch ready, the most stable vessel on the seven seas, the one with all the lifeboats. If only I could give orders to the moon—make it full, and order the stars to come out. For I really should travel by night. That's the safest thing. Safety first, I always say. I better bring a little money along, just in case. But where shall we go? Canada perhaps, or the United States.

OFFICER   Just wait a little while. Don't lose heart.

A WOUNDED SOLDIER *staggers on*.

DUNCAN   What's that drunk doing here?

OFFICER   He's not drunk. He's wounded.

DUNCAN   If you come from the battle, give me a report. Who's won?

SOLDIER   Does it matter?

OFFICER   Who's won? Was there a winner? You're in the presence of your king.

DUNCAN   I am your sovereign—the Archduke Duncan.

SOLDIER   Oh, I'm sorry, sir. I'm a bit wounded. I've been stabbed and shot. (*He staggers.*)

DUNCAN   It's no good pretending to faint. Answer me! Was it them or us?

SOLDIER   I'm not sure. It all got a bit too much for me. To tell you the truth, I left early. Before the end.

DUNCAN   You should have stayed.

OFFICER   Then he wouldn't be here to answer your questions.

DUNCAN   He left "before the end" as if it was a boring play.

SOLDIER   I fell down. Passed out. Came round again. Got up as best I could and, as best I could, dragged myself here.

DUNCAN (*to the* SOLDIER)   Are you sure you're one of ours?

SOLDIER   Who do you mean, "ours"?

21

OFFICER   The Archduke's and the Archduchess's, of course. They're standing right here in front of you.

SOLDIER   I didn't see you on the battlefield, my lord.

DUNCAN (*to the* SOLDIER)   What were your generals' names?

SOLDIER   I don't know. I was just coming out of the pub and a sergeant on horseback lassoed me. My mates were lucky. They got away. I tried to resist, but they hit me over the head, tied me up and carried me off. They gave me a sword. Oh, I seem to have dropped it somewhere. And a pistol. (*He puts the pistol to his head and pulls the trigger.*) Out of ammunition. Must have fired it all. There were a load of us out there on the field and they made us shout "Long live Glamiss and Candor."

DUNCAN   Traitor, you're one of our enemies.

OFFICER   I shouldn't cut his head off if I were you, my lord. Not if you want to hear the rest.

SOLDIER   And then they shot at us, and we shot at them.

DUNCAN   Who's "they"?

SOLDIER   And then they took us prisoner. And then they told me if you want to keep a head on your shoulders, you'd better join us. They told us to shout "Down with Candor, down with Glamiss." And then we shot at them and they shot at us. I was hit several times, wounded in the thigh, and then I guess I fell down. Then I woke up and the battle was still going on a long way away. There was nothing but heaps of dying men all around me. So, as I said I started walking; and my right leg is hurting, and my left leg is hurting, and I'm losing blood from the wound in my thigh. And then I got here . . . That's all I've got to say—except that I'm still bleeding. (*Gets up painfully. Totters.*)

DUNCAN   This idiot's made me none the wiser.

SOLDIER   That's all I've got to say. I don't know any more.

DUNCAN (*to* LADY DUNCAN)   He's a deserter.

LADY DUNCAN *draws her dagger. Her arm is poised to stab the* SOLDIER.

SOLDIER   Oh, don't bother yourself ma'am. (*He gestures off right.*) I'll just crawl over to that tree there and kick off. You can save yourself the trouble. (*He goes staggering off, left.*)

LADY DUNCAN   At least he's polite. Unusual for a soldier.

From the right, the noise of a body falling.

DUNCAN (*to the* OFFICER)   Stay here and defend me. I may need you. (*To* LADY DUNCAN) Quickly, take one of the horses, trot up to the front, then come back and tell me what's going on. Don't get too near though. I'll look through my telescope.

LADY DUNCAN *goes out right. While* DUNCAN *is looking through his telescope, we can see* LADY DUNCAN *upstage on her horse. Then* DUNCAN *folds up his telescope.*

Meanwhile, the OFFICER *has been standing with his sword drawn, looking menacingly in all directions.* DUNCAN *goes out right followed by the* OFFICER *carrying the armchair.*

Scene: near the battlefield.

Shouts of "Victory! Victory! Victory! . . ." coming from downstage left and right.

The word "victory" is repeated, modulated, orchestrated until the end of the following scene.

Sound of a horse galloping closer and closer is heard from the wings right. An ORDERLY *hurries on left.*

ORDERLY (*shading his eyes*)   Is that a horse? I think it's coming nearer. Yes. It's coming toward us at full tilt.

BANCO (*comes on from left and shades his eyes*)   I wonder what the rider wants, galloping so fast on that magnificent stallion. It must be a messenger.

ORDERLY   It's not a man. It's a woman.

> *Sound of neighing. The hoof beats stop.* LADY DUNCAN *appears, a riding crop in her hand.*

BANCO   It's her Highness, the Archduchess, the Archduchess. I humbly greet your highness. (*He bows, then kneels to kiss the Archduchess's hand.*) What is your Highness doing so near the battlefield? We're proud and happy that your Highness takes such an interest in our silly squabbles. As for our own life, we hold it at a pin's fee, but we are worried about your Highness's safety.

LADY DUNCAN   Duncan has sent me for news. He wants to know what's going on and whether you've won the war.

BANCO   I understand his impatience. We *have* won.

LADY DUNCAN   Bully for you. Rise, my dear Macbett.

BANCO I'm not Macbett. I'm Banco.

LADY DUNCAN Excuse me. Rise, my dear Banco.

BANCO Thank you, madam. (*To the* ORDERLY) What are you gaping at? Get the hell out of here, you stupid bastard.

ORDERLY Yessir. (*He disappears.*)

BANCO I apologize for that momentary indiscretion. Swearing like a trooper. Please forgive me, your Highness.

LADY DUNCAN Of course I forgive you, Banco. It's to be expected in wartime. People are more high strung than in peacetime, obviously. The main thing is to win. If a few rude words are going to help the war effort, that's fine by me. Have you taken Baron Candor prisoner?

BANCO Of course.

LADY DUNCAN And Baron Glamiss?

MACBETT'S VOICE (*coming from the left*) Banco. Banco. Where are you? Who are you talking to?

BANCO To her Highness, Lady Duncan, sent by the Archduke himself to gather information. Macbett will tell you about the fate of Glamiss.

MACBETT (*still offstage*) I'll be right with you.

BANCO I'll leave you to Macbett, madam. He'll tell you what's happening to our prisoners and give you a full account.

MACBETT'S VOICE (*quite near now*) I'm coming.

BANCO Excuse me, your Highness. I must go and feed my men. A good general is like a mother to his troops. (*He goes out left.*)

MACBETT'S VOICE (*nearer still*) Coming. Coming.

MACBETT *enters left. He greets* LADY DUNCAN.

MACBETT We have served our beloved sovereign well. Candor is in our hands. We've pursued Glamiss to a nearby mountain which you can see in the distance there. He's surrounded. We've got him trapped.

LADY DUNCAN So you're General Macbett, are you?

MACBETT At your command, your Highness.

LADY DUNCAN I remember you looking different. You don't look very much like yourself.

MACBETT My face looks different when I'm tired and I'm afraid I don't look very much like myself. People often take me for my twin brother. Or for Banco's twin brother.

LADY DUNCAN You must get tired quite a lot.

MACBETT War isn't a picnic. But one must learn to take the rough with the smooth. Let's say it's . . .

LADY DUNCAN *puts her hand to* MACBETT *who kneels and kisses it, then gets up quickly.*

. . . an occupational hazard.

LADY DUNCAN I'll go and tell the Archduke the good news.

BANCO'S VOICE (*in the wings*) All clear.

LADY DUNCAN *goes to the wings stage right and signals with her hand. She returns center stage. Fanfares are heard.*

MACBETT His Highness the Archduke!

SOLDIER His Highness the Archduke!

BANCO'S VOICE The Archduke!

LADY DUNCAN Here comes the Archduke!

BANCO'S HEAD (*appearing and disappearing*) The Archduke!

SOLDIER   The Archduke!

MACBETT   The Archduke!

LADY DUNCAN   Here comes the Archduke!

BANCO'S VOICE   The Archduke!

SOLDIER   The Archduke!

MACBETT   The Archduke!

LADY DUNCAN   Here comes the Archduke!

BANCO'S HEAD   The Archduke!

SOLDIER   The Archduke!

MACBETT   The Archduke!

LADY DUNCAN   Here comes the Archduke!

Blazing fanfares. The sound of cheering. DUNCAN *enters right. The fanfares stop.*

LADY DUNCAN   The battle is over.

MACBETT   Greetings, your Highness.

BANCO'S HEAD   Greetings, your Highness.

SOLDIER   Greetings, your Highness.

MACBETT   My humble greetings.

DUNCAN   Did we win?

MACBETT   The danger is over.

DUNCAN   Thank God. Has Candor been executed?

MACBETT   No, my good lord. But we've taken him prisoner.

DUNCAN   Why haven't you killed him? What are you waiting for?

MACBETT   Your orders, my good lord.

DUNCAN   You have them. Off with his head. Jump to it. What have you done with Glamiss? Have you torn him limb from limb?

MACBETT   No, my good lord. But he is surrounded.

Any moment now we'll take him prisoner. There's no cause for alarm, your Majesty.

DUNCAN Well then, well done. I can't thank you enough.

The SOLDIERS *and the crowd shouting "Hurrah!" We don't see them—unless they're projected onto the back.*

MACBETT We're proud and happy to have been of service, my good lord.

BANCO'S HEAD (*appearing and disappearing*) We were only doing our duty, my good lord.

More fanfares which get softer and softer until they become a background accompaniment to the scene.

DUNCAN Thank you, my dear generals, and thank you, my gallant soldiers, who saved my country and my throne. Many of you laid down your lives in the struggle. Thank you all again, dead or alive, for having defended my throne . . . which, of course, is also yours. When you return home, whether it be to your humble villages, your lowly hearths, or your simple but glorious tombs, you will be an example to generations to come, now and in the future and, better still, in the past; they will keep your memory alive for hundreds and hundreds of years, in word and deed, voiceless perhaps but ever present, in fame or anonymity, in the face of an undying yet transient history. Your presence, for even though absent you will be present to those who, whether they can see you or not, shall gaze lovingly at your photographs—your presence will serve as a pointer, tomorrow, and in the future, to all those who are tempted not to follow your example. As for the present, continue as you have done in the past, to earn your daily bread as gallantly as ever by the sweat of your brow, neath the sun's burning rays and under the watchful eye of your lords and masters who love you despite yourselves and whatever your shortcomings have a higher opinion of you than you might imagine. You may go.

Fanfares and hurrahs fainter now.

MACBETT   Bravo!

SOLDIER   Bravo!

DUNCAN   Nicely put, don't you think?

LADY DUNCAN   Bravo, Duncan! (*She applauds.*) That was a marvelous speech.

MACBETT *and the* SOLDIER *applaud.*

BANCO'S VOICE   Bravo!

DUNCAN   They deserved it. In future, my generals and my friends will all share in my glory. And my noble wife. (*He smiles at* LADY DUNCAN *and kisses her hand.*) You can all be proud of yourselves. And now, justice and retribution. Bring in Candor. Where's Banco?

MACBETT   He's with the prisoner.

DUNCAN   He will be the executioner.

MACBETT (*aside*)   That honor should have been mine.

DUNCAN   Let him approach with the traitor. Go and get him.

> *The* SOLDIER *goes out left. At the same moment* CANDOR *and* BANCO *come on right. Banco's head is covered in a hood. He is wearing a red pullover and carrying an axe.* CANDOR *is handcuffed.*

DUNCAN (*to* CANDOR)   You're going to pay for your treachery.

CANDOR   And pay dearly. I have no illusions. If only I had won. The victor is always right. *Vae victis.* (*To* MACBETT) If you'd fought for me, I'd have rewarded you well. I'd have made you a duke. And you, Banco, I'd have made you a duke, too. You'd both have been loaded with honor and riches.

DUNCAN (*to* CANDOR)   Don't worry. Macbett will be Baron Candor. He'll inherit all your lands, and your wife and daughter, too, if he likes.

MACBETT (*to* DUNCAN)   I'm faithful to you, my lord. I'm faithfulness personified. I was born faithful to you, as a dog or horse is born faithful to its master.

DUNCAN (*to* BANCO)   Don't you worry, either. You've no need to be jealous. Once Glamiss is captured and beheaded, you will be Baron Glamiss and inherit all his property.

MACBETT (*to* DUNCAN)   Thank you, my lord.

BANCO (*to* DUNCAN)   Thank you, my lord.

MACBETT (*to* DUNCAN)   We would have been faithful.

BANCO (*to* DUNCAN)   We would have been faithful.

MACBETT   Even if you hadn't rewarded us.

BANCO   Even if you hadn't rewarded us.

MACBETT   Serving you is its own reward.

BANCO   Serving you is its own reward.

MACBETT   But as it is, your bounty well satisfies our natural greed.

BANCO   We thank you from the bottom of our heart.

MACBETT *and* BANCO (MACBETT *drawing his sword and* BANCO *brandishing his cleaver*)   . . .   from the bottom of our heart. We'd go through Hell for you, your gracious Majesty.

> A MAN *crosses the stage from left to right.*

MAN   Rags and bones! Rags and bones.

DUNCAN (*to* CANDOR)   You see how devoted *they* are?

MACBETT *and* BANCO   It's because you are a good king, generous and just.

MAN   Rags and bones! Rags and bones. (*He goes out left. The rag-and-bone* MAN *can be cut or kept in as the director wishes.*)

> As he goes out, a SERVANT *comes in carrying armchairs for* DUNCAN, LADY DUNCAN *and the others.*
>
> *During the action which follows, he will bring a towel, a basin, and some soap, or perhaps just some eau de cologne for* LADY DUNCAN, *who washes her hands—very emphatically, as if trying to get rid of a spot or stain. She should do this in a rather mechanical absent-minded way. Then the same* SERVANT *brings in a table and tea service and serves cups of tea to those present.*
>
> *The lights come up on a guillotine, and then gradually a whole forest of guillotines comes into view.*

DUNCAN (*to* CANDOR) Have you anything to say? We're listening.

They all settle down to look and listen.

SERVANT (*to* LADY DUNCAN) Tea is served, madam.

CANDOR If I'd been stronger, I'd have been your anointed king. Defeated, I'm a traitor and a coward. If only I'd won. But History was against me. History is right, objectively speaking. I'm just a historical dead end. I hope at least that my fate will serve as an example to you all and to posterity. Throw in your lot with the stronger. But how do you know who the stronger is, before it comes to the crunch? The masses should keep out of it until the fighting is over and then throw in their lot with the winner. The logic of events is the only one that counts. Historical reason is the only reason. There are no transcendental values to set against it. I am guilty. But our rebellion was necessary, if only to prove that I'm a criminal. I shall die happy. My life is an empty husk. My body and those of my followers will fertilize the fields and push up wheat for future harvests. I'm a perfect example of what not to do.

DUNCAN (*quietly to* LADY DUNCAN) This is too long. Aren't you bored? I bet you're excited to see what happens next. No, no, we won't torture him. Just put him to death. Disappointed? I've got a surprise for you, dear. The entertainment will be more lavish than you thought. (*To everybody*) Justice demands that the soldiers of Candor's army be executed along with him. There aren't very many of them.

137,000—not too many, not too few. Let's get a move on. We want to be done by dawn.

> *Upstage a large red sun slowly sinks.* DUNCAN *claps his hands.*

Go on. Off with his head.

CANDOR   Long live the Archduke!

> BANCO *has already arranged his head on the guillotine. To do so he has had to get rid of his ax.*
>
> *One after another,* CANDOR's *soldiers pass in a continuous procession to the guillotine. (The same actors follow each other around.)*
>
> *Another way to do it would be to have the scaffold and the guillotine appear as soon as* DUNCAN *gives the order.* BANCO *pushes the button and the heads fall.*

BANCO   Hurry, hurry, hurry, hurry!

> *After each "Hurry" the blade falls. The heads pile up in the basket.*

DUNCAN (*to* MACBETT)   Have a seat next to my dear wife.

> MACBETT *sits down beside* LADY DUNCAN. *They both need to be clearly visible so that the audience can see what's going on. For example,* LADY DUNCAN *and the others could be sitting with their*

backs to the guillotine but still appear to be watching the executions. LADY DUNCAN *is counting heads.*

During the whole of this, the SERVANT *is serving tea to one or other of the characters, offering them buns and so on.*

MACBETT I'm overwhelmed, madam, to be so close to you.

LADY DUNCAN (*still counting*) Four, five, six, seven, seventeen, twenty-three, thirty-three, thirty-three— I think I missed one.

Without ever stopping counting, she starts nudging MACBETT *and playing footsy with him—at first discreetly, then more and more obviously until the whole thing becomes excessive and grossly indecent.*

MACBETT *edges away a little. At first he is rather embarrassed and confused. Then gradually, half-frightened, half-pleased, he gives in, eagerly acquiescing.*

DUNCAN (*to* MACBETT) Now, back to business. I create you Baron Candor. Your comrade Banco will be Baron Glamiss when Glamiss has been executed in his turn.

LADY DUNCAN (*still fondling* MACBETT) A hundred and sixteen, a hundred and eighteen, what a moving sight.

MACBETT I'm very grateful to your Highness, my lord.

LADY DUNCAN   Three hundred. I'm getting dizzy. Nine thousand three hundred.

DUNCAN (*to* MACBETT)   Now listen carefully.

> MACBETT *disentangles himself a little from* LADY DUNCAN, *who continues to play with him, rubbing up against him and putting her hand on his knee.*

MACBETT   I'm all ears, my lord.

DUNCAN   I shall keep half of Candor's lands and half of Glamiss's too. They will be added to the crown estates.

LADY DUNCAN   Twenty thousand.

BANCO (*still working the guillotine*)   Thank you, your Highness.

DUNCAN (*to* MACBETT)   There are some things you will have to do for me—both of you—in return. Certain duties, certain obligations, certain taxes to be paid.

> An OFFICER *runs onstage and stops center stage.*

OFFICER   Glamiss has escaped!

DUNCAN   I'll tell you the details later.

OFFICER   My lord, Glamiss has escaped.

DUNCAN (*to the* OFFICER)   What?

OFFICER   Glamiss has escaped. Part of his forces rallied to him.

> BANCO *stops guillotining and comes downstage. The other characters jump up.*

BANCO How could he have escaped? He was surrounded. He was as good as taken. It's a conspiracy.

DUNCAN Damn!

LADY DUNCAN (*still pressing against* MACBETT) Damn!

MACBETT Damn!

DUNCAN (*to* BANCO) Whoever is responsible, you won't be Baron Glamiss nor get half his lands till you bring him before me bound hand and foot. (*Turning to the* OFFICER.) And you're going to have your head cut off for bringing us such disagreeable news.

OFFICER It's not my fault.

> A SOLDIER *drags the* OFFICER *upstage to the guillotine. The* OFFICER *yells. They cut his head off.*

> *Music.* DUNCAN *goes out.* LADY DUNCAN *plays footsy with* MACBETT *and rolls her eyes at him.*

> DUNCAN *comes back on. The music stops.*

> *He addresses* LADY DUNCAN *who is going out backward blowing kisses to* MACBETT.

DUNCAN Come along, madam. (*He drags her off by the scruff of the neck.*)

LADY DUNCAN I wanted to see what was going to happen next.

DUNCAN'S VOICE (*to* BANCO) Bring me Glamiss—by tomorrow.

> *Music.*

BANCO (*going over to* MACBETT) We've got to start all over again. What a disaster.

MACBETT   What a disaster.

BANCO   What a disaster.

MACBETT   What a disaster.

Wind and storm.

The stage is dark. All we can see is Macbett's face—and the faces of the FIRST AND SECOND WITCHES *when they appear.*

Enter MACBETT *and* BANCO

MACBETT   What a storm, Banco. Terrifying. The trees look as if they're trying to pull themselves up by the roots. I just hope they don't topple onto our heads.

BANCO   It's ten miles to the nearest inn and we haven't got a horse.

MACBETT   We didn't realize how far we'd come.

BANCO   And now we're caught in the storm.

MACBETT   Still, we can't stand here all day discussing the weather.

BANCO   I'll go and stand by the road. Perhaps a cart will come along and give us a lift.

MACBETT   I'll wait for you here.

BANCO *goes out.*

FIRST WITCH   Hail Macbett, thane of Candor.

MACBETT   You frightened me. I didn't know there was anybody there. It's only an old woman. She looks like a witch to me. (*To the* WITCH) How did you know I'm thane of Candor? Has rumor added it's murmur to the rustling of the forest? Are wind and storm echoing the news abroad?

SECOND WITCH (*to* MACBETT) Hail Macbett, thane of Glamiss.

MACBETT Thane of Glamiss? But Glamiss lives. Besides, Duncan promised his title and his lands to Banco. (*He notices that it was the* SECOND WITCH *who spoke.*) Another one.

FIRST WITCH Glamiss is dead. Drowned. The torrent swept him and his horse away.

MACBETT Is this some kind of joke? I'll have your tongues cut out, you old hags.

FIRST WITCH Duncan is very displeased with Banco for letting Glamiss escape.

MACBETT How do you know?

SECOND WITCH Duncan wants to take advantage of this. He is going to give you the title and keep the lands for himself.

MACBETT Duncan is loyal. He keeps his promises.

FIRST WITCH You will be Archduke and rule the country.

MACBETT You're lying. I'm not ambitious. Or rather my only ambition is to serve my king.

FIRST WITCH You will be king yourself. It is ordained. I can see the star on your forehead.

MACBETT It's impossible. Duncan has a son, Macol, who's studying at Carthage. He is the natural and legitimate heir to the throne.

SECOND WITCH There's another son who's just finishing a post-graduate degree in economics and navigation at Ragusa. He's called Donalbain.

MACBETT Never heard of him.

FIRST WITCH (*to* MACBETT) You can forget about him. He won't interfere. (*To the* SECOND WITCH) It wasn't navigation. It was business studies—though obviously shipping was part of the course.

MACBETT Rubbish. Die. (*He waves his sword and strikes at the air. We hear the Witches' terrifying laughter.*) Hellish creatures.

They have disappeared.

Did I really see them and hear them? They've changed into the wind and storm. Disappeared into the roots of trees.

FIRST WITCH (*now a woman's melodious voice*) I'm not the wind. I'm not a dream, Macbett. I'll soon be back. Then you'll know my power and my charm.

MACBETT Jumping catfish! (*He takes three or four more swipes, then stops.*) I thought I recognized that voice. Who can it be? Voice, have you a body? Have you a face? Where are you?

FIRST WITCH (*melodiously*) Right beside you. Right beside you. And a long way off. Farewell, Macbett. Till we meet again.

MACBETT I'm shivering. It must be the cold. Or the rain. Or is it fear? Or horror? Or some mysterious longing that this voice arouses in me? Am I already under its spell? (*Change of tone.*) Filthy hags. (*Change of tone.*) Banco. Banco. Where can he have got to? Have you found a cart? Where are you? Banco. Banco. (*He goes out right.*)

Pause. The stage is empty. Noise of the storm.

FIRST WITCH (*to the* SECOND WITCH) Here comes Banco.

SECOND WITCH When they're not together, they're either following each other about or looking for each other.

The FIRST WITCH *hides stage right. The* SECOND WITCH *hides stage left.* BANCO *enters upstage.*

BANCO Macbett. Macbett. (*He makes a show of looking for* MACBETT.) Macbett, I've found the cart. (*To himself*) I'm soaked to the skin. Luckily, it's slackening off a bit.

In the distance a voice calling "Banco."

I thought I heard him calling. He should have stayed here. He must have got tired of waiting.

VOICE Banco! Banco!

BANCO Here I am. Where are you?

VOICE (*nearer now, coming from the right*) Banco! Banco!

BANCO Coming. Where are you? (*He runs stage right.*)

ANOTHER VOICE (*different, coming from the left*) Banco!

BANCO Where are you?

FIRST WITCH'S VOICE Banco!

BANCO Is that Macbett?

SECOND WITCH'S VOICE Banco!

BANCO It doesn't sound like him.

The TWO WITCHES *leave their hiding place and close in on* BANCO *from both sides.*

BANCO   What's the meaning of this?

FIRST WITCH   Hail Banco, Macbett's companion.

SECOND WITCH   Hail, General Banco.

BANCO   Who are you? Hideous creatures, what do you want? Lucky for you, you're women—of a kind. Otherwise, I'd have cut your heads off for fooling with me like that.

FIRST WITCH   Now don't get excited, General Banco.

BANCO   How do you know my name?

SECOND WITCH   Hail Banco—who won't be thane of Glamiss.

BANCO   How do you know that title was supposed to be mine? How do you know I won't get it? Has rumor added its murmur to the rustling of the forest? Are wind and storm echoing the news abroad?—Anyway, I can't be thane of Glamiss.

FIRST WITCH   Glamiss is dead. Drowned. The torrent swept him and his horse away.

BANCO   Is this some kind of joke? I'll have your tongues cut out, you old hags.

SECOND WITCH   Duncan is very displeased with you for letting Glamiss escape.

BANCO   How do you know?

FIRST WITCH   He wants to take advantage of this. He's going to give the title, Baron Glamiss, to Macbett. All the estates will revert to the crown.

BANCO   The title alone would have been enough. Why should Duncan wish to deprive me of it? No, Duncan is loyal. He keeps his promises. Why should he give the title to Macbett. Why should he punish me? Why should Macbett have all the favors and all the privileges?

SECOND WITCH   Macbett is your rival. Your successful rival.

BANCO   He is my companion. He is my friend. He is my brother. He is loyal.

The WITCHES *withdraw a little and jump up and down.*

THE TWO WITCHES   He thinks he's loyal. He thinks he's loyal. (*They laugh.*)

BANCO (*drawing his sword*)   Monstrous creatures, I know who you are. You're spies. You're working for the enemies of Duncan, our loyal and beloved sovereign.

He tries to run them through. But they escape and run off, FIRST WITCH *to the left,* SECOND WITCH *to the right.*

FIRST WITCH (*before she disappears*)   Macbett will be king. He'll take Duncan's place.

SECOND WITCH   He'll mount the throne.

BANCO *runs backward and forward brandishing his sword, trying to run them through.*

BANCO   Where are you? Accursed gypsies. Hellish creatures. (*He sheathes his sword and returns to center stage.*) Did I really see them and hear them?

They've changed into the wind and storm. They've changed into the roots of trees. Was it all a dream?

SECOND WITCH'S VOICE   Hear me, Banco, hear me. (*The* SECOND WITCH'S VOICE *becomes pleasant and melodious*.) Mark me. You won't be king. But you'll be greater than Macbett. Greater than Macbett. You will found a dynasty which will rule over our country for a thousand years. You will be greater than Macbett—root and father of many kings.

BANCO   I don't believe it . . . I don't believe it. (*He takes three or four more swipes, then stops*.) I thought I recognized that voice. Who can it be? Voice, have you a body? Have you a face? Where are you?

VOICE   Right beside you. And a long way off. You'll see me again soon. Then you'll know my power and my charm. Till then, Banco.

BANCO   I'm shivering. It must be the rain. Or is it fear? Or horror? Or some mysterious longing that this voice arouses in me? Who does it remind me of? Am I already under its spell? (*Change of tone*.) Just ugly old hags, that's all. Spies, intriguers, liars. Father of kings, me? When our beloved sovereign has sons of his own? Macol, who's studying at Carthage, is the natural and legitimate heir to the throne. There's also Donalbain who's just finished a post-graduate degree in business studies at Ragusa. Nonsense, every word of it. I won't give it another thought.

MACBETT'S VOICE   Banco! Banco!

BANCO   It's Macbett's voice. Macbett! Ah, there you are.

MACBETT'S VOICE   Banco!

BANCO Macbett! (*He rushes off left, where* MAC-
BETT'S VOICE *was coming from.*)

Pause. The stage is empty.

*Gradually, the light changes. Upstage a sort of enor-
mous moon, very bright, surrounded by big stars. Perhaps the Milky Way, too, like a big bunch of grapes.*

*During the next scene the setting will gradually become
more specific. Little by little we are able to make out
the outline of a castle. In the middle of it, a small
lighted window. It's important that the sets work with
or without the characters.*

*The following sequence can be kept in or cut as re-
quired.*

DUNCAN *crosses silently right to left.*

When he's gone off left, LADY DUNCAN *appears and follows him across. She disappears.*

MACBETT *crosses silently, going the opposite way. An*
OFFICER *crosses silently from right to left.*

BANCO *crosses silently right to left.*

A WOMAN *crosses slowly and silently in the opposite
direction. (I think the woman, at least, should be kept
in.)*

Pause. The stage is empty. BANCO *enters upstage.*

BANCO Well, how about that then? The witch was
right. Where did she get her information? Does she

have a contact at court? But so quickly. Perhaps she does have supernatural powers after all. Unusual, to say the least. Perhaps she's found a way of harnessing sound waves. Perhaps she's discovered that channel, mentioned in certain myths, that enables you to put the person talking in touch with the person listening. Perhaps she's invented mirrors which reflect distant images as if they were close at hand, as if they were talking to you six feet away. Perhaps she has enchanted glasses that enable her to see for hundreds or thousands of miles. Perhaps she has instruments for amplifying sound and making the ear incredibly sensitive. One of the Archduke's officers has just come to tell me of Glamiss's death and of my being passed over. Did Macbett plot to gain the title? Could my loyal friend and companion be a swindler? Is Duncan so ungrateful that he can disregard my efforts and the risks I've taken, the dangers I've undergone to defend him and keep him from harm? Is there no one I can trust? And shall I then suspect my brother, my faithful dog, the wine I drink, the very air I breathe? No, no. I know Macbett too well to be anything but convinced of his loyalty and his virtue. Duncan's decision is undoubtedly his own; no prompter but his own nature. It shows him in his true colors. But Macbett can't have heard yet. When he does, he'll refuse to have anything to do with it. (*He begins to go off left, then returns center stage.*) They have looked into space, these monstrous daughters of the devil. Can they also look into the future? They told me I should father a line of kings. Strange and incredible. I wish they could tell me more. Perhaps they really do know what will happen. I wish I could see them but I can't . . . But I did.

He goes out left. MACBETT *enters right. Before he comes on we hear him shouting.*

MACBETT   Banco! Banco! (*He comes on. Shouts again, and again.*) Banco! Where can he have got to? They told me he was hereabouts. I wanted to talk to him. A messenger from the Archduke has summoned me to court. The king tells me Glamiss is dead and that I'm to inherit his title, but not his lands. The witches' prophecies are beginning to come true. I tried to tell Duncan that I didn't want him to dispossess Banco in my favor. I tried to tell him that Banco and I were friends and that Banco hadn't done anything to deserve such treatment, that he had served his sovereign loyally. But he wouldn't listen, hear me. If I accept the title, I might lose the friendship of my dear comrade, Banco. If I refuse, I shall incur the king's displeasure. Have I the right to disobey him? I don't disobey when he sends me to war, so I can't very well disobey when he rewards me. That would be contempt. I must explain to Banco. Anyway, Baron Glamiss—it's only a title. There's no money in it, since Duncan's annexed the lands. Yes, I should like to see Banco, but at the same time perhaps I'd rather wait. It's a tricky situation. How did the witches know about it? Will their other predictions come true? It seems impossible. I'd like to know the logic behind it. How do they explain a chain of cause and effect which will set me on the throne? I'd like to hear what they have to say about it—if only to make fun of them. (*He goes out left.*)

Pause. The stage is empty.

The BUTTERFLY HUNTER *comes on left, butterfly net in hand. He is wearing a pale-colored suit and a boater. He has a little black mustache and pince nez. He chases a couple of butterflies and runs off left in pursuit of a third.*

BANCO (*enter right*)   Where are those witches? They prophesied Glamiss's death. That's come true. They told me I'd be dispossessed of my rightful title, Baron Glamiss. They told me I should father a long line of kings and princes. Will their prophecy about my descendants come true as well? I'd like to know the logic behind it. How do they explain the chain of cause and effect that will set my posterity on the throne? I'd like to know what they have to say about it—if only to make fun of them. (*He goes out left.*)

Pause. The stage is empty. MACBETT *comes on left. The* FIRST WITCH *has taken up her position stage right unseen by the audience.*

FIRST WITCH (*to* MACBETT. *She speaks in a croaking voice.*)   Macbett, you wanted to see me.

Lights up on the WITCH. *She is dressed like a witch, bent double, with a rasping voice. She props herself up on a big stick. She has dirty white unkempt hair.*

MACBETT *jumps. His hand goes instinctively to his sword.*

MACBETT   Cursed hag. You were there all the time.
FIRST WITCH   I came when you called.
MACBETT   On the battlefield I've never been afraid. No enemy has ever frightened me. Bullets have whizzed past my head. I've hacked my way through burning forests. When the flagship was sinking, I wasn't afraid. I jumped into the shark-infested sea and slashed their throats with one hand while swimming with the other. But my hair stands on end when I see this woman's shadow or hear her voice. There's a smell of sulphur in the air. I must use my sword— but as a cross not as a weapon. (*To the* WITCH) You guessed I wanted to speak with you.

The SECOND WITCH *appears behind the* FIRST WITCH *during the following exchange. There needs to be a certain distance—not very great— between them.*

The SECOND WITCH *will need to move slowly from stage left to stage right to arrive in the center of the spot, behind the* FIRST WITCH.

The FIRST WITCH *appears suddenly. A spot comes up on her. The* SECOND WITCH *should emerge more slowly into the light, first of all her head, then her shoulders, then the rest of her body, and her stick. Her shadow enlarged by the lighting will be thrown on the back wall.*

FIRST WITCH   I heard you. I can read your thoughts. I know what you're thinking now and what was going through your mind a few moments ago. You pretended you wanted to see me to make fun of me. You admitted you were afraid. Pull yourself together, general, for Hell's sake. What do you want to know?

MACBETT   Don't you know already?

FIRST WITCH   Some things I know, but some things are beyond my power. Our knowledge is limited, but I can see that, whether you are aware of it or not, your ambition has been kindled. Whatever explanations you may give yourself they are false; they only conceal your true intent.

MACBETT   I want only one thing; to serve my sovereign.

FIRST WITCH   Who are you kidding?

MACBETT   You want to make me believe that I'm other than I am—but you won't succeed.

FIRST WITCH   You're useful to him, otherwise he'd have your head.

MACBETT   My life is his to dispose of.

FIRST WITCH   You're his instrument. You saw how he got you to fight against Glamiss and Candor.

MACBETT   He was right. They were rebels.

FIRST WITCH   He took all Glamiss's lands and half of Candor's.

MACBETT   Everything belongs to the king. Equally the king and all he has belong to us. He is looking after it for us.

FIRST WITCH   And his flunkeys are left to carry the can.

SECOND WITCH   He, he, he, he, he!

MACBETT (*noting the* SECOND WITCH) Where did she spring from?

FIRST WITCH He doesn't know how to hold an ax. He doesn't know how to use a scythe.

MACBETT What do you know about it?

FIRST WITCH He can't fight himself—he sends others out to do it for him.

SECOND WITCH He'd be too frightened.

FIRST WITCH He knows how to steal other people's wives.

SECOND WITCH Are they part of the public domain too —the King's property?

FIRST WITCH He demands service from others, although he doesn't know the meaning of the word himself.

MACBETT I didn't come here to listen to your treasonous lies.

FIRST WITCH Why did you come and meet me, if that's all we're good for?

MACBETT I'm beginning to wonder. It was a mistake.

FIRST WITCH Then bugger off . . .

SECOND WITCH If you're not interested . . .

FIRST WITCH You hesitate, I see. So you've decided to stay.

SECOND WITCH If you'd rather . . .

FIRST WITCH If it's easier for you . . .

SECOND WITCH We can disappear.

MACBETT Stay a little, daughters of Satan. I want to know more.

FIRST WITCH Be your own master, instead of taking someone else's orders.

SECOND WITCH Tools he's done with he casts aside. You've outlived your usefulness.

FIRST WITCH   He despises those who are faithful to him.

SECOND WITCH   He thinks they're cowards.

FIRST WITCH   Or fools.

SECOND WITCH   He respects those who stand up to him.

MACBETT   He fights them, too. He beat the rebels Glamiss and Candor.

FIRST WITCH   Macbett beat them, not he.

SECOND WITCH   Glamiss and Candor were his faithful generals before you.

FIRST WITCH   He hated their independence.

SECOND WITCH   He took back what he'd given them.

FIRST WITCH   A fine example of his generosity.

SECOND WITCH   Glamiss and Candor were proud.

FIRST WITCH   And noble. Duncan couldn't stand that.

SECOND WITCH   And courageous.

MACBETT   I won't be another Glamiss. Or another Candor. This time there won't be a Macbett to beat them.

FIRST WITCH   You're beginning to understand.

SECOND WITCH   He, he, he, he!

FIRST WITCH   If you're not careful, he'll have time to find another.

MACBETT   I behaved honorably. I obeyed my sovereign. That's a law of heaven.

SECOND WITCH   It wasn't behaving honorably to fight your peers.

FIRST WITCH   But their death will be useful to you.

SECOND WITCH   He would have used them against you.

FIRST WITCH   Now nothing stands in your way.

SECOND WITCH   You want the throne. Admit it.

MACBETT   No.

FIRST WITCH   It's no good pretending you don't. You're worthy to be king.

SECOND WITCH   You're made for it. It's written in the stars.

MACBETT   You open the slippery slope of temptation before me. Who are you and what do you want? I almost succumbed to your wiles. But I came to my senses in time. Away.

The TWO WITCHES *give ground.*

FIRST WITCH   We're here to open your eyes.

SECOND WITCH   We only want to help you.

FIRST WITCH   It's for your own good.

SECOND WITCH   Justice is all we ask.

FIRST WITCH   True justice.

MACBETT   Stranger and stranger.

SECOND WITCH   He, he, he, he!

MACBETT   Have you really got my interests at heart? Does justice mean so much to you? You old hags, ugly as sin, you shameless old women want to sacrifice your life for my happiness?

SECOND WITCH   Yes, yes, he, he, he, of course.

FIRST WITCH   Because we love you, Macbett. (*Her voice is beginning to alter.*)

SECOND WITCH   It's because she loves you—(*The voice alters.*)—as much as her country, as much as justice, as much as the commonwealth.

FIRST WITCH (*melodious voice*)   It's to help the poor. To bring peace to a country that has known such suffering.

MACBETT   I know that voice.

FIRST WITCH   You know us, Macbett.

MACBETT For the last time, I order you to tell me who you are or I'll cut your throats for you. (*Taking out sword.*)

SECOND WITCH Save yourself the trouble.

FIRST WITCH All in good time, Macbett.

SECOND WITCH Put back your sword.

MACBETT *submits.*

And now, Macbett, I want you to watch closely, very closely. Open your eyes. Pin back your ears.

The SECOND WITCH *circles the* FIRST WITCH *like a conjuror's assistant. Each time she circles, she jumps two or three times. These jumps develop into a gracious dance as the new aspects of the* TWO WITCHES *are unveiled. Toward the end the dance becomes slow.*

SECOND WITCH (*circling the first*) Quis, quid, ubi . . . quibus auxiliis, cur, quomodo, quando. Felix qui potuit regni cognoscere causas. Fiat lux hic et nunc et fiat voluntas tua. Ad augusta per angusta, ad augusta per angusta. (*The* SECOND WITCH *takes the* FIRST WITCH's *stick and throws it away.*) Alter ego surge, alter ego surge.

The FIRST WITCH, *who was bent double, straightens up.*

For this scene—a transformation scene—the FIRST WITCH *is center stage, brilliantly lit.*

The SECOND WITCH *as she circles passes alternately through light and dark areas, depending on whether she is downstage or upstage of the* FIRST WITCH.

MACBETT, *standing to one side, is in the shade. We are vaguely aware of his startled reactions as the scene progresses.*

The SECOND WITCH *uses her stick like a magic wand. Each time she touches the* FIRST WITCH *with her wand a transformation takes place.*

Obviously the whole scene should be done to music. For the beginning at least some staccato would be most suitable.

SECOND WITCH (*as before*) Ante, apud, ad, adversus . . .

She touches the FIRST WITCH *with her wand. The* FIRST WITCH *lets fall her old cloak. Underneath is another old cloak.*

Circum, circa, citra, cis . . .

She touches the FIRST WITCH, *who sheds her old cloak. She is still covered by an ancient shawl that reaches to her feet.*

SECOND WITCH Cotra, erga, extra, infra . . . (*The* SECOND WITCH *stands up straight.*) Inter, intra, juxta, ob . . . (*As she passes in front of the* FIRST WITCH *she pulls off her glasses.*) Penes, pone, post et praeter . . . (*She pulls off the old shawl. Underneath the shawl a very beautiful dress appears, covered in spangles and glinting stones.*) Prope, propter, per, secundum . . . (*Music more legato and melodious. She pulls off the First Witch's pointed chin.*) Supra, versus, ultra, trans . . .

> *The* FIRST WITCH *sings several notes and trills. The light is sufficiently bright for us to see the First Witch's face and mouth as she sings. She stops singing. The* SECOND WITCH, *as she passes behind the* FIRST, *throws away her stick.*

Video, meliora, deteriora sequor.

MACBETT (*trancelike*) Video meliora, deteriora sequor.

> *The* SECOND WITCH *keeps circling.*

MACBETT *and* FIRST WITCH (*together*) Video meliora, deteriora sequor.

FIRST *and* SECOND WITCHES Video meliora, deteriora sequor.

ALL THREE (*together*) Video meliora, deteriora sequor. Video meliora, deteriora sequor. Video meliora, deteriora sequor.

> *The* SECOND WITCH *removes what's left of the First Witch's mask—i.e., the pointed nose and hairpiece.*

> *Still circling, she puts a scepter in the First Witch's hands and a crown on her head. Under the lights the* FIRST WITCH *appears as if surrounded in a halo of light.*

> *As she passes behind, the* SECOND WITCH *removes her face mask and her old clothes in a single go.*

Now revealed in all her beauty, the FIRST WITCH *becomes* LADY DUNCAN.

The SECOND WITCH *becomes her lady in waiting, equally young and beautiful.*

MACBETT   Oh your Majesty. (*He falls to his knees.*)

The SECOND WITCH, *now Lady Duncan's maid, places a step ladder behind the* FIRST WITCH, *now* LADY DUNCAN, *for her to climb.*

If this can't be managed, LADY DUNCAN *walks backward, slowly and majestically, stage right, where there is a ladder which she proceeds to mount.*

MACBETT *gets up and once more throws himself at Lady Duncan's feet.*

MACBETT   Oh mirabile visu! Oh madam!

In one movement, the LADY IN WAITING *tears off Lady Duncan's sumptuous dress.* LADY DUNCAN *stands revealed in a sparkling bikini, a black-and-red cape on her back and holding a scepter in one hand and in the other a dagger which the* LADY IN WAITING *has given her.*

LADY IN WAITING (*pointing to* LADY DUNCAN)   In naturalibus.

MACBETT   Let me be your slave.

LADY DUNCAN (*to* MACBETT, *holding out the dagger to him*)   I'll be yours if you wish. Would you like that? Here is the instrument of your ambition and our rise to power. (*Seductively.*) Take it if that's what you want, if you want me. But act boldly. Hell helps those who help themselves. Look into yourself. You can feel your desire for me growing, your hidden ambition coming into the open, inflaming you. You'll take his place at my side. I'll be your mistress. You'll be my sovereign. An indelible bloodstain will mark this blade—a souvenir of your success and a spur to greater things which we shall accomplish with the same glory. (*She raises him up.*)

MACBETT   Madam, sire, or rather siren . . .

LADY DUNCAN   Still hesitating, Macbett?

LADY IN WAITING (*to* LADY DUNCAN)   Make up his mind for him.

LADY DUNCAN   Make up your mind.

MACBETT   Madam, I have certain scruples . . . can't we just . . .

LADY DUNCAN   I know you're brave. But even brave men have their weaknesses and moments of cowardice. Above all they suffer from guilt—and that's mortal. Pull yourself together. You were never afraid to kill when someone else was giving the orders. If fear now weighs you down, unburden yourself to me. I'll reassure you, promise you that no man of woman born will be able to conquer you. No other army will defeat your army till the forest arms itself to march against you.

LADY IN WAITING   Which is practically impossible. (*To* MACBETT) Remember we want only to save our country. The two of you will build a better society, a brave new world.

The stage grows gradually darker.

MACBETT *rolls at Lady Duncan's feet. All that can be seen is Lady Duncan's glistening body. We hear the voice of the* LADY IN WAITING.

LADY IN WAITING   Omnia vincit amor.

Blackout.

A room in the palace.

In front of the palace, BANCO *and an* OFFICER.

OFFICER   His Highness is tired. He can't see you now.

BANCO   Does he know what I've come for?

OFFICER   I explained everything, but he says it's a *fait accompli*. He's given Glamiss's title to Macbett and he can't very well take it back again. Besides, it's only his word.

BANCO   But still . . .

OFFICER   That's the way it is.

BANCO   Does he know Glamiss is dead, drowned?

OFFICER   I told him, but he'd already heard. Lady Duncan knew of it through her Lady in Waiting.

BANCO   There's no reason why he shouldn't give me my promised reward. The title or the lands, if not both.

OFFICER   What do you want me to do? I've done my best?

BANCO   It's impossible. He can't do this to me.

    Enter DUNCAN *stage right.*

DUNCAN (*to* BANCO) What's all the fuss about?

BANCO My lord—

DUNCAN I don't like being disturbed. What do you want?

BANCO Didn't you tell me, that when Glamiss had been taken, dead or alive, you'd give me my reward?

DUNCAN Where is he? Dead or alive I don't see him.

BANCO You know very well he's drowned.

DUNCAN That's hearsay. Bring me his body.

BANCO His bloated corpse has been swept out to sea.

DUNCAN Well go and look for it. Take a boat.

BANCO The sharks have eaten it.

DUNCAN Take a knife and cut through the shark's belly.

BANCO Several sharks.

DUNCAN Cut through all their bellies then.

BANCO I risked my life defending you against the rebels.

DUNCAN You've come out of it alive, haven't you?

BANCO I killed all your enemies.

DUNCAN You had that pleasure.

BANCO I could've done without it.

DUNCAN But you didn't

BANCO My lord—

DUNCAN Not another word. Where is Glamiss's body? Show me the *corpus delicti.*

BANCO Glamiss's death is common knowledge. You've given his title to Macbett.

DUNCAN Are you demanding an explanation?

BANCO It's not fair.

DUNCAN I'll be the judge of that. We'll find other rebel barons to dispossess. There's bound to be something for you in the future.

BANCO   I'm afraid I think you're lying.

DUNCAN   How dare you insult me?

BANCO   But . . . but . . .

DUNCAN   Show this gentleman the door.

The OFFICER *appears to be on the point of launching himself violently at* BANCO. *He shouts.*

OFFICER   Out!

DUNCAN   No need for rough stuff. Banco is a good friend of ours. His nerves are a little on edge, that's all. He'll get over it. He'll get his opportunity.

BANCO (*going out*)   What a bloody sauce . . .

DUNCAN (*to the* OFFICER)   I don't know what got into me. I should have made him Baron. But he wanted the money, too, which should rightfully have reverted to me. Well, that's the way it is. But if he gets dangerous, we shall have to be careful—very careful.

OFFICER (*putting his hand on his sword*)   I understand, my lord.

DUNCAN   No, no, not so fast. Not immediately. Later. If he becomes dangerous. Would you like his title and half his lands?

OFFICER (*energetically*)   Yes, my lord. Whatever you say, my lord.

DUNCAN   You're a thrusting little codger, aren't you? I suppose you'd like me to confiscate Macbett's title and fortune and give you a bit of that as well?

OFFICER (*as before*)   Yes, my lord. Whatever you say, my lord.

DUNCAN   Macbett is also becoming dangerous. Very dangerous. Perhaps he'd like to replace me on the throne. That sort of person needs to be watched.

Hoodlums, that's what they are, gangsters. All they think about is money, power, luxury. I wouldn't be surprised if Macbett also had an eye on my wife. Not to mention my courtesans. How about you? Would you like me to lend you my wife?

OFFICER (*protesting energetically*) Oh no, my lord.

DUNCAN Don't you fancy her?

OFFICER She is very beautiful, my lord. But honor, your honor comes first.

DUNCAN That's a good chap. Thanks. I'll see that you're rewarded.

OFFICER Whatever you say, my lord.

DUNCAN I'm surrounded by grasping enemies and fickle friends. Nobody is unselfish. You'd think the prosperity of the kingdom and my personal well-being would satisfy them. They've got no ideals. None at all. We shall be on our guard.

Fanfares and music. Something old fashioned and formal.

A room in the Archduke's Palace. Just a few items, one or two chairs and a different backcloth, will do to establish the locality. Whatever can be set up in a blackout lasting not more than thirty seconds.

Music. DUNCAN enters right, followed by LADY DUNCAN. He is agitated and she has difficulty keeping up with him.

DUNCAN comes to a sudden halt center stage. He turns to LADY DUNCAN.

DUNCAN   No. madam, I won't allow it.

LADY DUNCAN   So much the worse for you.

DUNCAN   I said, I won't allow it.

LADY DUNCAN   Why not? Why ever not?

DUNCAN   Let me speak frankly, with my customary candor.

LADY DUNCAN   Frankly or not it all boils down to the same thing.

DUNCAN   What do I care?

LADY DUNCAN   You said I could. It's no good denying it.

DUNCAN   I shall if I want. I said perhaps.

LADY DUNCAN   What about me? What am I supposed to say?

DUNCAN   Whatever comes into your head.

LADY DUNCAN   I never say whatever comes into my head.

DUNCAN   If it isn't in your head how can you say it?

LADY DUNCAN   First one thing, then another. Tomorrow it'll be something else again.

DUNCAN   I can't help that.

LADY DUNCAN   Neither can I.

DUNCAN   Stop contradicting.

LADY DUNCAN   You're always putting things off.

DUNCAN   You've only yourself to blame.

LADY DUNCAN   You're such an old fuss-pot.

DUNCAN   Madam, madam, madam!

LADY DUNCAN   You're being very stubborn. Men are so self-centered.

DUNCAN   Let's get back to the subject in hand.

LADY DUNCAN   It's no good your getting cross, it only makes me cross as well. The most important thing is done. If you were more objective about it . . . but you aren't. So, let's leave it. It's all your fault.

DUNCAN Hold your tongue, madam. He who laughs last, laughs longest.

LADY DUNCAN Your obsessions, your *idées fixes*.

DUNCAN That'll do.

LADY DUNCAN So you still refuse . . .

DUNCAN You'll regret it.

LADY DUNCAN You can't make an omelette without breaking eggs.

DUNCAN You'll pay dearly.

LADY DUNCAN Are you threatening me?

DUNCAN From top to toe.

LADY DUNCAN Another threat!

DUNCAN One day you'll go too far.

LADY DUNCAN And another!

DUNCAN I won't have it. No, absolutely not. You just wait. The shoe will be on the other foot. I'll tell him. You see if I don't. I'll rub his nose in it.

DUNCAN *goes out quickly, followed by* LADY DUNCAN.

LADY DUNCAN I'll forestall you, Duncan. By the time you find out it'll be too late.

DUNCAN, *still agitated, has gone out left after his last speech.* LADY DUNCAN *follows him out, almost at a run.*

The scene between the two of them should be played as a violent quarrel.

MACBETT *and* BANCO *enter right.* MACBETT *looks worried. He has a serious air about him.*

MACBETT No, seriously. I thought Lady Duncan was a shallow woman. I was wrong. She is capable of deep feeling. She is so vivacious, energetic. She really is. And intellectual. She has some very profound views on the future of mankind: though she's by no means a utopian dreamer.

BANCO It's possible. I believe you. It's difficult to get to know people, but once they've opened their hearts to you . . . (*Pointing to Macbett's belt.*) That's a handsome dagger that you've got there.

MACBETT A gift from her. Anyway, I'm glad to have had a chance to talk with you at long last after all this chasing about like a dog after its own tail or the devil chasing his shadow.

BANCO You can say that again.

MACBETT She's unhappily married. Duncan is a brute. He maltreats her. It's very trying. She's very delicate, you know. And he's peevish and broody. Lady Duncan is like a child—she likes to sport and amuse herself, play tennis, make love. Of course, it's none of my business, really.

BANCO Of course.

MACBETT Far be it from me to speak ill of the king or want to run him down.

BANCO Perish the thought.

MACBETT The Archduke is a very good man, loyal and . . . generous. You know how fond I am of him.

BANCO Me, too.

MACBETT All in all he's a perfect monarch.

BANCO Almost perfect.

MACBETT Obviously, as far as perfection is possible in this world. It's a perfection that doesn't exclude certain imperfections.

BANCO An imperfect perfection. But perfection all the same.

MACBETT Personally, I've got nothing against him—though my own opinion doesn't enter into it. He has the good of the country at heart. Yes, he's a good king. Though he should be more appreciative of his impartial advisers—like you, for example.

BANCO Or you.

MACBETT Like you or me.

BANCO Quite.

MACBETT He's a bit autocratic.

BANCO Very autocratic.

MACBETT A real autocrat! Nowadays autocracy isn't always the best way to govern. That's what Lady Duncan thinks anyway. She's very charming, you know, and has a lot of interesting ideas, two qualities that aren't often found together.

BANCO Not often, no.

MACBETT She could give him some good advice, interesting advice, get him to see . . . to understand certain principles of government which, in an impartial way, she would share with us. We ourselves, of course, being quite impartial.

BANCO All the same we've got to live, earn our daily bread.

MACBETT Duncan understands that.

BANCO Yes, he's shown himself very understanding so far as you're concerned. He's showered you with blessings.

MACBETT I didn't ask him to. He paid, he paid well, well more or less—he didn't pay too badly for the services I rendered him—which it was my duty to render, since he is my feudal overlord.

BANCO   He didn't pay me at all! As you know. He took Glamiss's lands for himself and gave you the title.

MACBETT   I don't know what you're referring to. Duncan do a thing like that? Never—well, hardly ever—well, not very often. He has his lapses. I didn't intrigue for it, I promise.

BANCO   I never said you did. I know it's not your fault.

MACBETT   It's not my fault. Listen: perhaps we can do something for you. We—Lady Duncan and I that is—we could advise him. We could, for example, advise him to take you on as his adviser.

BANCO   Lady Duncan knows about this, does she?

MACBETT   She's very concerned about you. She's very upset by the king's thoughtlessness. She wants to make it up to you. She's already put in a word for you with the Archduke, you know. I suggested it to her, and she agreed. We've both intervened on your behalf.

BANCO   Why keep on if your attempts have been unsuccessful?

MACBETT   We'll use other arguments. More cogent ones. Then perhaps he'll understand. If not . . . we'll try again. With even stronger arguments.

BANCO   Duncan is stubborn.

MACBETT   Very stubborn. Stubborn . . . (*He looks left and right.*) . . . as stubborn as a mule. Still, even the stubbornest mule can be made to budge.

BANCO   Made to, yes.

MACBETT   Fair enough, he's given me the estates—but he's reserved the right to hunt on my lands. Apparently, it's for "state expenses."

BANCO   So he says . . .

MACBETT   He *is* the state.

BANCO   My estates are still the same as ever and he takes from me ten thousand chickens a year and their eggs.

MACBETT   You should complain.

BANCO   I fought for him at the head of my own personal army. Now he wants to merge it with his army. He wants to turn my own men against me.

MACBETT   And me.

BANCO   My ancestors would turn over in their graves . . .

MACBETT   So would mine! And there's all his cronies and parasites.

BANCO   Who fat themselves on the sweat of our brow.

MACBETT   And our chickens.

BANCO   And our sheep.

MACBETT   And our pigs.

BANCO   The swine.

MACBETT   And our bread.

BANCO   The blood we've shed for him.

MACBETT   The dangers we've undergone.

BANCO   Ten thousand chickens, ten thousand horses, ten thousand recruits. What does he do with them? He can't eat them all. The rest just goes bad.

MACBETT   And a thousand young girls.

BANCO   We know what he does with them.

MACBETT   He owes us everything.

BANCO   More than he can pay.

MACBETT   Not to mention the rest.

BANCO   My honor.

MACBETT   My glory.

BANCO   Our ancestral rights.

MACBETT   My property.

BANCO   The right to make more and more money.

MACBETT   Self-rule.

BANCO   To run our own affairs.

MACBETT   We must drive him out.

BANCO   Lock, stock and barrel. Down with Duncan.

MACBETT   Down with Duncan!

BANCO   We must overthrow him.

MACBETT   I was going to suggest . . . we should divide the kingdom. We'll each have our share and I'll take the throne. I'll be king and you can be my chamberlain.

BANCO   Your second-in-command.

MACBETT   Well third, actually. It's a difficult task we've set ourselves and we need all the help we can get. There is a third in this conspiracy—Lady Duncan.

BANCO   Well, well. That's a piece of luck.

MACBETT   She's indispensable.

LADY DUNCAN *enters upstage.*

BANCO   Madam! What a surprise.

MACBETT (*to* BANCO)   We're engaged.

BANCO   The future Lady Macbett. Well, well. (*Looking from one to the other.*) Heartiest congratulations. (*He kisses Lady Duncan's hand.*)

LADY DUNCAN   To the death!

They all three draw their daggers and cross them at arm's length.

Let's swear to kill the tyrant!

MACBETT   The usurper.

BANCO   Down with the dictator!

LADY DUNCAN   The despot.

MACBETT   He's a miscreant.

BANCO   An ogre.

LADY DUNCAN   An ass.

MACBETT   A goose.

BANCO   A louse.

LADY DUNCAN   Let's swear to exterminate him.

ALL THREE (*together*)   We swear to exterminate him.

Fanfares. The conspirators go out quickly left.

The ARCHDUKE comes on right. In this scene, at least at the beginning, DUNCAN has real majesty.

Enter the OFFICER upstage.

OFFICER   My lord, it's the first day of the month, the day when the scrofulous, the tubercular, the consumptive, and the hysterical come for you to cure their maladies by your heavenly gift.

A MONK comes on left.

MONK   Greetings, my lord.

DUNCAN   Greetings, father.

MONK   God be with you.

DUNCAN   And with you.

MONK   May the lord preserve you. (*He blesses the Archduke, who bows his head.*)

The OFFICER, carrying the king's purple robe, the crown, and the royal scepter, goes over to the MONK.

The MONK *blesses the crown and takes it from the* OFFICER. *He goes over to* DUNCAN, *who kneels down, and puts it on his head.*

MONK   In the name of Almighty God, I confirm you in your sovereign power.

DUNCAN   May the lord make me worthy.

The OFFICER *gives the purple cloak to the* MONK *who puts it around Duncan's shoulders.*

MONK   May the Lord bless you and keep you, and may no harm come to you so long as you wear this cloak.

A SERVANT *comes on right carrying the ciborium for communion. He gives it to the* MONK *who offers* DUNCAN *the Host.*

DUNCAN   Domine non sum dignus.

MONK   Corpus Christi.

DUNCAN   Amen.

The MONK *gives the ciborium back to the* SERVANT, *who goes out.*

The OFFICER *hands the* MONK *the scepter.*

MONK   I renew the gift of healing which the Lord God transmits through me, his unworthy servant. May the Lord purge our souls as he heals the sickness of our feeble bodies. May He cure us of jealousy, pride, luxury, our base striving after power, and may He open our eyes to the vanity of worldly goods.

DUNCAN   Hear us, O Lord.

OFFICER (*kneeling*)   Hear us, O Lord.

MONK   Hear us, O Lord. May hatred and anger waft away like smoke in the wind. Grant that man may prevail against nature, where suffering and destruction reign. May love and peace be freed from their chains, may all destructive forces be chained up that joy may shine forth in heavenly light. May that light flood us that we may bathe ourselves in it. Amen.

DUNCAN *and* OFFICER   Amen.

MONK   Take your scepter with my blessing. With it you are to touch the sick.

> DUNCAN *and the* OFFICER *get up. The* MONK *kneels before* DUNCAN *who mounts the throne and sits. The* OFFICER *stands on Duncan's left. This scene should be played with solemnity.*

DUNCAN   Bring in the patients.

> The MONK *rises and goes and stands on Duncan's right.*

> The FIRST SICK MAN *comes in upstage left. He is bent double and walks with difficulty. He is wearing a cape with a hood. His face is a ravaged mask —like a leper's.*

Come here. A little nearer. Don't be afraid.

> The SICK MAN *approaches and kneels on one of the bottom steps of the throne. He has his back to the audience.*

FIRST SICK MAN   Have pity on me, my lord. I've come a long way. On the other side of the ocean, there is a continent and beyond that continent, there are seven countries. And beyond those seven countries there's another sea, and beyond that sea there are mountains. I live on the other side of those mountains in a damp and sunless valley. The damp has eaten away my bones. I'm covered in scrofula, in tumors and pustules which break out everywhere. My body is a running sore. I stink. My wife and children can't bear me to come near them. Save me, lord. Cure me.

DUNCAN   I shall cure you. Believe in me and hope. (*He touches the Sick Man's head with his scepter.*) By the grace of our Lord Jesus Christ, by the gift of the power vested in me this day, I absolve you of the sin which has stained your soul and body. May your soul be as pure as clear water, as the sky on the first day of creation.

The FIRST SICK MAN *stands up and turns toward the audience. He draws himself up to his full height, drops his stick and lifts his hands to heaven.*

His face is clear and smiling. He shouts for joy and runs out left.

The SECOND SICK MAN *enters right and approaches the throne.*

DUNCAN   What is your trouble?

SECOND SICK MAN   My lord, I'm unable to live and I can't die. I can't sit down, I can't lie down, I can't stand still, and I can't run. I burn and itch from the top of my head to the soles of my feet. I can't bear to be indoors or on the street. For me, the universe is a prison. It pains me to look at the world. I can't bear the light nor sit in the shade. Other people fill me with horror, yet I can't bear to be alone. My eyes wander restlessly over trees, sheep, dogs, grass, stars, stones. I have never had a single happy moment. I should like to be able to cry, my lord, and to know joy. (*During this speech, he has come up to the throne and climbed the steps.*)

DUNCAN   Forget you exist. Remember that you are.

Pause.

Seen from behind, one can read in the twitching of the Sick Man's shoulders that it's impossible for him to comply.

I order you. Obey.

The SECOND SICK MAN, *who was twisted in agony, relaxes his back and shoulders and appears to be calming down. He gets up slowly, holds out his arms and turns around. The audience can see the contorted face relax and light up.*

He walks off left, jauntily, almost dancing.

OFFICER   Next!

A THIRD SICK MAN *approaches* DUNCAN, *who cures him in the same way. Then in quick succession a Fourth, Fifth, Sixth . . . Tenth, Eleventh come on stage right and go out left after having been touched by Duncan's scepter.*

Before each entrance, the OFFICER *shouts "Next!"*

Some of the Patients are on crutches or in wheel-chairs.

All this should be properly controlled and toward the end should be accompanied by music which gradually gets faster and faster.

While this is going on, the MONK *has slowly dropped away till he is sitting rather than kneeling on the floor. He looks poised.*

After the Eleventh SICK MAN, *the tempo becomes slower and the music fades into the distance.*

Two last patients come in, one from the left, the other from the right. They are wearing long capes with hoods that come down over their faces. The OFFICER *who shouted "Next" fails to notice the last patient, who creeps up behind him.*

Suddenly the music cuts out. At the same moment, the MONK *throws back his hood or takes off his mask, and we see that it's* BANCO *in disguise. He pulls out a long dagger.*

DUNCAN (*to* BANCO)   You?

At the same moment, LADY DUNCAN *throws off her disguise and stabs the* OFFICER *in the back. He falls.*

DUNCAN (*to* LADY DUNCAN)   You, madam?

*The other beggar—*MACBETT—*also pulls out a dagger.*

DUNCAN Murderers!
BANCO (*to* DUNCAN) Murderer!
MACBETT (*to* DUNCAN) Murderer!

DUNCAN *dodges* BANCO *and comes face to face with* MACBETT. *He tries to go out left but his escape is cut off by* LADY DUNCAN, *who holds out her arms to stop him. She has a dagger in one hand.*

LADY DUNCAN (*to* DUNCAN) Murderer!
DUNCAN (*to* LADY DUNCAN) Murderess! (*He runs left, meets* MACBETT.)
MACBETT Murderer!
DUNCAN Murderer! (*He runs right.* BANCO *cuts him off.*)
BANCO (*to* DUNCAN) Murderer!
DUNCAN (*to* BANCO) Murderer!

DUNCAN *backs toward the throne. The three others close in on him, slowly drawing their circle tighter.*

As DUNCAN *mounts the first step,* LADY DUNCAN *snatches off his cloak.* DUNCAN *backs up the steps trying to cover his body with his arms. Without his cloak he feels naked and exposed.*

He doesn't get very far, however, for the others are after him. His scepter falls one way, his crown the other. MACBETT *pulls at him and brings him down.*

DUNCAN   Murderers!

He rolls on the ground. BANCO *strikes the first blow, shouting.*

BANCO   Murderer!
MACBETT (*stabbing him a second time*)   Murderer!
LADY DUNCAN (*stabbing him a third time*)   Murderer!

The three of them get up and stand over him.

DUNCAN   Murderers! (*Quieter.*) Murderers! (*Feebly.*) Murderers!

The three conspirators draw apart. LADY DUNCAN *stays by the body, looking down.*

LADY DUNCAN   He was my husband, after all. Now that he's dead, he looks just like my father. I couldn't stand my father.

Blackout.

A room in the palace. In the distance we can hear the crowd shouting, "Long live Macbett! Long live his bride! Long live Macbett! Long live his bride!"

Two SERVANTS *enter upstage, one from one side, one from the other. They meet downstage center. They can be played by two men, or a man and a woman, possibly even two women.*

SERVANTS *(looking at each other)* They're coming.

> *They go and hide upstage. Enter left Duncan's widow, the future* LADY MACBETT, *followed by* MACBETT. *They have not as yet acquired the regal attributes.*
>
> *The cheering and shouts of "Long live Macbett and his bride" are louder.*
>
> *They go to the exit stage left.*

LADY DUNCAN Thank you for bringing me to my apartments. I'm going to lie down. I'm quite tired after my exertions.

MACBETT   Yes, you could do with a rest. I'll come and pick you up at ten o'clock for the marriage ceremony. The coronation is at midday. In the afternoon, at five o'clock, there will be a banquet—our wedding feast.

LADY DUNCAN (*giving her hand to* MACBETT *to be kissed*)   Till tomorrow then, Macbett.

She goes out. MACBETT *crosses to go out right. The sound of scattered cheering.*

The two SERVANTS *who had hidden reappear and come downstage.*

FIRST SERVANT   Everything is ready for the wedding ceremony and the breakfast afterward.

SECOND SERVANT   Wines from Italy and Samoa.

FIRST SERVANT   Bottles of beer coming by the dozen.

SECOND SERVANT   And gin.

FIRST SERVANT   Oxen.

SECOND SERVANT   Herds of deer.

FIRST SERVANT   Roebuck to be barbecued.

SECOND SERVANT   They've come from France, from the Ardennes.

FIRST SERVANT   Fishermen have risked their lives to provide sharks. They'll eat the fins.

SECOND SERVANT   They killed a whale for oil to dress the salad.

FIRST SERVANT   There'll be Pernod from Marseille.

SECOND SERVANT   Vodka from the Urals.

FIRST SERVANT   A giant omelette containing a hundred and thirty thousand eggs.

SECOND SERVANT   Chinese pancakes.

FIRST SERVANT   Spanish melons from Africa.

SECOND SERVANT   There's never been anything like it.

FIRST SERVANT   Viennese pastries.

SECOND SERVANT   Wine will flow like water in the streets.

FIRST SERVANT   To the sound of a dozen gypsy orchestras.

SECOND SERVANT   Better than Christmas.

FIRST SERVANT   A thousand times better.

SECOND SERVANT   Everyone in the country will get two hundred and forty-seven black sausages.

FIRST SERVANT   And a ton of mustard.

SECOND SERVANT   Frankfurters.

FIRST SERVANT   And sauerkraut.

SECOND SERVANT   And more beer.

FIRST SERVANT   And more wine.

SECOND SERVANT   And more gin.

FIRST SERVANT   I'm drunk already, just thinking about it.

SECOND SERVANT   Just thinking about it I can feel my belly bursting.

FIRST SERVANT   My liver swelling. (*They throw their arms around each other's necks and stagger out drunkenly, shouting "Long live Macbett and his bride."*)

BANCO *enters right. He crosses to stage center and stops, facing the audience. He appears to reflect for a moment.* MACBETT *appears upstage left.*

MACBETT   Ah, it's Banco. What's he doing here all by himself? I'll hide and overhear him. (*He pretends to pull invisible curtains.*)

BANCO   So Macbett is to be king; Baron Candor, Baron

Glamiss, then king—as from tomorrow. One by one
the witches' predictions have come true. One thing
they didn't mention was the murder of Duncan, in
which I had a hand. But how would Macbett have
come to power unless Duncan had died or abdicated
in his favor—which is constitutionally impossible?
You have to take the throne by force. Another thing
they didn't mention was that Lady Duncan would be
Lady Macbett. So Macbett gets everything—while I
get nothing. What an extraordinarily successful
career—wealth, fame, power, a wife. He's got everything a man could possibly want. I struck down Duncan because I had a grudge against him. But what
good has it done me? True, Macbett has given me his
word. He said I could be chamberlain. But will he
keep his promise? I doubt it. Didn't he promise to be
faithful to Duncan—and then kill him? People will
say I did the same. I can't say I didn't. I can't get it
out of my mind. I'm sorry now—and I haven't any of
Macbett's advantages, his success, his fame, to stifle
my remorse. The witches told me I shouldn't be
archduke or king, but they said I should father a
whole line of kings, princes, presidents, and dicta-
tors. That's some consolation. They said it would
happen, yes, they said it would happen. They've
proved conclusively that they can see into the future.
Before I met them I had no desire, no ambition beyond that of serving my king. Now I'm consumed
with envy and jealousy. They've taken the lid off my
ambition and here I am carried away by a force I
can't control—grasping, avid, insatiable. I shall
father dozens of kings. That's something. But yet
I have no sons or daughters. And I'm not married.

Whom shall I marry? The Lady in Waiting is rather sexy. I'll ask her to marry me. She's a bit spooky but so much the better. She'll be able to see danger coming and we can take steps to avoid it. Once I'm married, once I've started a family, once I'm chamberlain, I'll curtail Macbett's powers. I'll be his *éminence gris*. Who knows, perhaps the witches will reconsider their predictions. Perhaps I will reign in my own lifetime after all. (*He goes out right.*)

MACBETT   I heard every word, the traitor! So that's all the thanks I get for promising to make him chamberlain. I didn't know my wife and her maid had told him that he'd be father to a line of kings. Funny she never mentioned it. It's disturbing to think she kept it from me. Who are they trying to fool, me or Banco? Why? Banco father to a line of kings. Have I killed Duncan to put Banco's issue on the throne? It's all a sinister plot. Well, we'll soon see about that. We'll soon see if my initiative can foil the snares of destiny the devil has set for me. Let's destroy his issue at the fountainhead—that is, Banco himself. (*He crosses right and calls.*) Banco! Banco!

BANCO'S VOICE   Coming, Macbett. Coming. (BANCO *comes on.*) What do you want?

MACBETT   Coward, so that is how you repay me for all the favors I was going to grant you. (*He stabs* BANCO *in the heart.*)

BANCO (*falling*)   Oh my God! Have mercy.

MACBETT   Where are all those kings now? They're going to rot with you and in you, nipped in the bud. (*He goes.*)

Blackout.

Lights up.

Shouts of "Long live Macbett! Long live Lady Macbett! Long live our beloved king! Long live the bride!"

MACBETT *and* LADY MACBETT *come on right. They are in robes of state. They wear crowns and purple robes.*

MACBETT *is carrying his scepter. Sound of bells ringing and the enthusiastic cheering of the crowd.* MACBETT *and* LADY MACBETT *stop center stage with their backs to the audience and wave left and right to the crowd.*

Noise of the crowd: "Hurrah! Long live the Archduke! Long live the Archduchess!"

MACBETT *and* LADY MACBETT *turn and salute the audience, waving and blowing kisses. They turn and face each other.*

MACBETT   We'll discuss it later.
LADY MACBETT   I can explain everything, dear.
MACBETT   Well, I've canceled your prediction. I've nipped it in the bud. You've no longer got the upper

hand. I discovered your little arrangements and took steps accordingly.

LADY MACBETT I didn't mean to hide anything from you, love. As I said, I can explain everything. But not in public.

MACBETT We'll discuss it later.

> MACBETT *takes her hand and they go out right, smiling at the crowd. The cheering continues.*
>
> *Pause. The stage is empty.* LADY MACBETT *comes on with her* LADY IN WAITING. *She is in the same costume as in the previous scene.*

LADY IN WAITING It suits you, being a bride. The crowd cheering. The way you held yourself. Such grace. Such majesty. He cut a fine figure, too. He's looking much younger. You made a lovely couple.

LADY MACBETT He's gone to sleep. He had a few too many after the ceremony. And there's still the wedding feast to come. Let's make the most of it. Hurry up.

LADY IN WAITING Yes, ma'am. (*She collects a case from offstage right.*)

LADY MACBETT Away with this sacred and anointed crown. (*She throws the crown away. She takes off the necklace with a cross on it which she had been wearing.*) This cross has been burning me. I've got a wound, here on my chest. But I've doused it with curses.

> *Meanwhile the* LADY IN WAITING *has been opening the case and taking out her witch's costume. She proceeds to dress* LADY MACBETT *in it.*

The cross symbolizes the struggle of two forces, heaven and hell. Which will prove the stronger? Within this small compass a universal warfare is condensed. Help me. Undo my white dress. Quickly, take it off. It's burning me as well. And I spit out the Host which fortunately stuck in my throat. Give me the flask of spiced and magic vodka. Alcohol 90 proof is like mineral water to me. Twice I nearly fainted when they held up the icons for me to touch. But I carried it off. I even kissed one of them. Pouah, it was disgusting.

During all this, the LADY IN WAITING *is undressing her.*

Hurry up. I hear something.

LADY IN WAITING   Yes, ma'am. I'm doing my best.

LADY MACBETT   Hurry, hurry, hurry. Give me my rags, my smelly old dress. My apron covered in vomit. My muddy boots. Take this wig off. Where's my dirty gray hair? Give me my chin. Here, take these teeth. My pointed nose, and my stick tipped with poisoned steel.

The LADY IN WAITING *picks up one of the sticks left by the pilgrims.*

As LADY MACBETT *issues her orders, "Unhook my white dress!" etc., the* LADY IN WAITING *carries them out.*

As indicated in the text, she puts on her smelly old dress, her apron covered in vomit, her dirty gray hair, takes out her teeth, shows the plate to audience, puts on her pointed nose, etc.

FIRST WITCH   Hurry! Faster!

SECOND WITCH   I am hurrying, my dear.

FIRST WITCH   They are waiting for us.

The SECOND WITCH *produces a long shawl from the case and puts it around her shoulders, at the same time pulling on a dirty gray wig.*

The two WITCHES *are bent double and sniggering.*

I feel much more at home, dressed like this.

SECOND WITCH   He, he, he, he!

She shuts the case. They both sit astride it.

FIRST WITCH   Well, that's that, then.

SECOND WITCH   A job well done.

FIRST WITCH   We've mixed it nicely.

SECOND WITCH   He, he, he, he. Macbett won't be able to get out of it now.

FIRST WITCH   The boss will be pleased.

SECOND WITCH   We'll tell him all about it.

FIRST WITCH   He'll be waiting to send us on another mission.

SECOND WITCH   Let's skedaddle. Suitcase, fly!

FIRST WITCH   Fly! Fly! Fly!

The FIRST WITCH, *who is sitting in front of the case, mimes a steering wheel. It's a very noisy engine. The* SECOND WITCH *spreads her arms, like wings.*

Blackout. Spotlight on the case which appears to be flying.

The main hall of the palace. Upstage, the throne. Downstage and a little to the left, a table with stools. Four GUESTS *are already seated.*

Four or five life-size dolls represent the other GUESTS. *Upstage, other tables and other* GUESTS *projected onto the back wall on either side of the throne.*

MACBETT *comes on left.*

MACBETT   Don't get up, my friends.

FIRST GUEST   Long live the Archduke!

SECOND GUEST   Long live our sovereign!

THIRD GUEST   Long live Macbett!

FOURTH GUEST   Long live our guide! Our great captain! Our Macbett!

MACBETT   Thank you, friends.

FIRST GUEST   Glory and honor and health to our beloved sovereign, Lady Macbett!

FOURTH GUEST   Her beauty and her grace make her worthy of your highness. May you live and prosper. May the state flourish under your wise and powerful rule, guided and helped by your lady wife.

MACBETT   Accept my thanks for both. She should have been here by now.

SECOND GUEST   Her Highness is never late normally.

MACBETT   I left her only a few minutes ago. She and her maid were right behind me.

THIRD GUEST   Has she taken ill? I'm a doctor.

MACBETT   She's gone to her room to put on some lipstick, a dab of powder, and a new necklace. In the meanwhile, don't stop drinking. I'll come and join you.

A SERVANT *comes on.*

There's not enough wine. More wine there!

SERVANT   I'll go and get some, my lord.

MACBETT   Your health, my friends. How happy I am to be with you. I feel surrounded by the warmth of your affection. If you knew how much I need your friendship—as much as a plant needs water or a man wine. I find it consoling, soothing, reassuring, having you around me. Ah, if only you knew . . . But I mustn't let myself go. It's not the moment for confessions. You set out to do something and end up doing something quite different, which you didn't intend at all. History is full of tricks like that. Everything slips through your fingers. We unleash forces that we cannot control and which end up by turning against us. Everything turns out the opposite of what you wanted. Man doesn't rule events, events rule him. I was happy when I was serving Duncan faithfully. I hadn't a care in the world.

The SERVANT *comes in.* MACBETT *turns toward him.*

Quickly, we're dying of thirst. (*Looking at a portrait —it could just as easily be an empty frame.*) Who put Duncan's picture in my place? Is this someone's idea of a joke?

SERVANT   I don't know, my lord. I didn't see anything, my lord.

MACBETT   How dare you. (*He takes the* SERVANT *by the throat, then lets him go again. He goes to unhook the portrait—which could equally well be an empty frame or invisible.*)

FIRST GUEST   But that's your picture, my lord.

SECOND GUEST   They put your picture where Duncan's was, not vice versa.

MACBETT   It does look like him though.

THIRD GUEST   Your eyes are affected, my lord.

FOURTH GUEST (*to the* FIRST GUEST)   I wonder if myopia is brought on by power?

FIRST GUEST (*to the* FOURTH GUEST)   I shouldn't have thought so—not necessarily.

SECOND GUEST   Oh yes, it happens quite frequently.

As soon as MACBETT *lets go of his throat, the* SERVANT *goes off right.*

MACBETT   Perhaps I'm mistaken. (*To the others, who had got up at the same time as he did.*) Sit down, friends. A little wine will clear my head. Anyway, whoever it looks like, Duncan or me, let's smash that picture. Then we'll all have a few drinks. (*He sits down and drinks.*) Why are you looking at me like that? Sit down, I said. We'll all have a few drinks together. (*He stands up and pounds on the table with his fist.*) Sit down!

The GUESTS *sit down.* MACBETT *sits down too.*

Drink, gentlemen, drink. You must admit, I'm a better king than Duncan was.

THIRD GUEST   Hear, hear, my lord!

MACBETT   This country needs a younger man at the helm, braver and more energetic. I can assure you, you haven't lost in the exchange.

FOURTH GUEST   That's what we think, your Highness.

MACBETT   Think! What did you think of Duncan, when he was alive? Did you tell him what you thought? Did you tell him he was the bravest? The most energetic commander? Or did you tell him I should take his place? That I should be king instead of him?

FIRST GUEST   My lord—

MACBETT   I thought he was more suited to it myself. Do you agree? Or do you think differently? Answer me!

SECOND GUEST   My lord—

MACBETT   My lord, my lord, my lord . . . well, what then? You've lost your voice, have you? Anyone who thinks I'm not the best possible ruler, past, present and to come, get up and say so. You don't dare. (*Pause.*) You don't dare. And the greatest. And the most just. You miserable specimens. Go on, get drunk.

The lights go out upstage. The other lot of tables that were projected on the back or reflected by means of mirrors disappear.

BANCO *suddenly appears. When he starts speaking he is framed in the doorway, stage right. He moves forward.*

BANCO   I dare, Macbett.

MACBETT   Banco!

BANCO   I dare tell you you're a traitor, a swindler, and a murderer.

MACBETT (*giving ground*)   You're not dead after all.

The four GUESTS *have risen.* MACBETT *continues to give ground as* BANCO *comes forward.*

Banco! (*He half draws his dagger.*) Banco!

FIRST GUEST (*to* MACBETT)   It's not Banco, my lord.

MACBETT   I tell you it is.

SECOND GUEST   It's not Banco in flesh and blood. It's only his ghost.

MACBETT   His ghost? (*He laughs.*) Yes, it's only a ghost. I can see through it, put my hand through it. So you are dead after all. You don't frighten me. A pity I can't kill you a second time. This is no place for you here.

THIRD GUEST   He's come from Hell.

MACBETT   You've come from Hell and must return. How did you manage it? Show me the pass that Satan's lieutenant gave you. Have you got till midnight? Sit down. In the place of honor. Poor ghost. You can neither eat nor drink. Sit down among my guests here.

The GUESTS *are frightened and draw back.*

What are you worried about? Go up to him. Give him the illusion he exists. He'll despair even more when he returns to his dark abode . . . either too hot or too wet.

BANCO   Scum! All I can do now is curse you.

MACBETT   You can't make me feel any remorse. If I hadn't killed you first, you'd have killed me—as you did Duncan. You struck the first blow, remember? I was going to make you chamberlain, but you wanted to rule in my place.

BANCO   As you took Duncan's place, who made you Baron twice over.

MACBETT (*to the* GUESTS)   There's no cause for alarm. What are you so frightened of? To think I choose my generals from among these crybabies.

BANCO   I trusted you, I followed you, then you and the witches put a spell on me.

MACBETT   You wanted to substitute your progeny for mine. Well, you didn't get very far. All your children, your grandchildren, your great-grandchildren, died in your seed before being born. Why call me names? I just got there first, that's all.

BANCO   You're in for some surprises, Macbett. Make no mistake. You'll pay for this.

MACBETT   He makes me laugh. I say *he:* really all there is are a few odds and ends, the remains of his old personality—leftovers, a robot.

BANCO *disappears.*

At practically the same moment, DUNCAN *appears, mounting the throne.*

FOURTH GUEST   The Archduke! Look, look! The Archduke!

SECOND GUEST   The Archduke!

MACBETT   I'm the only Archduke around here. Look at me, can't you, when you speak to me.

THIRD GUEST   The Archduke! (*He points.*)

MACBETT (*turning*)   Is this some kind of reunion or something?

> *The* GUESTS *go cautiously up to* DUNCAN, *but stop a certain distance away. The* FIRST *and* SECOND GUESTS *kneel to the right and left of the throne. The two others, further off, are on either side of* MACBETT, *though a certain distance away.*

> *The three of them,* MACBETT *and the two* GUESTS, *have their backs to the audience. The first two are in profile.* DUNCAN, *on his throne, faces straight out.*

FIRST *and* THIRD GUESTS (*to the* ARCHDUKE)   My lord—

MACBETT   You didn't believe Banco was real, but you seem to believe that Duncan exists all right and is sitting there on the throne. Is it because he was your sovereign that you've grown used to paying him homage and holding him in awe? Now it's my turn to say, "It's only a ghost." (*To* DUNCAN) As you can see, I've taken your throne. And I've taken your wife. All the same, I served you well and you distrusted me. (*To his* GUESTS) Get back to your places. (*He draws his dagger.*) Quickly. You have no king here but me. You pay homage to me now.

> *The* GUESTS *retreat, terrified.*

And call me "My Lord." Say . . .

GUESTS (*bowing and scraping*)   We hear and obey, my lord. Our happiness is to submit.

FOURTH GUEST   Our greatest happiness is to do what you say.

MACBETT   I see you understand. (*To* DUNCAN) I don't want to see you again till you've been forgiven by the thousands of soldiers I slaughtered in your name, and till they have been pardoned in their turn by the thousands of women that they raped, and by the thousands of children and peasants they killed.

DUNCAN   I've killed or had killed tens of thousands of men and women, soldiers and civilians alike. I've had thousands of homesteads burnt to the ground. True. Very true. But there is one thing that you haven't got quite right. You didn't steal my wife. (*He laughs sardonically.*)

MACBETT   Are you mad? (*To the four* GUESTS) His death has made him balmy—isn't that right, gentlemen?

GUESTS (*one after the other*)   Yes, my lord.

MACBETT (*to* DUNCAN)   Go on, shoo! you silly old ghost.

DUNCAN *disappears behind the throne. He had already stood up to prepare his exit.*

MAID   My lord, my lord! She's disappeared!

MACBETT   Who?

MAID   Your noble wife, my lord. Lady Macbett.

MACBETT   What did you say?

MAID   I went into her room. It was empty. Her things were gone and so was her maid.

MACBETT   Go and find her and bring her to me. She had a headache. She's gone for a walk in the grounds to get a breath of fresh air before coming in to dinner.

MAID   We've looked everywhere. We've cried out her name. But only our echoes answered.

MACBETT (*to the four* GUESTS) Scour the forests! Scour the countryside! Bring her to me! (*To the* MAID) Go and look in the attic, in the dungeons, in the cellar. Perhaps she got shut in by mistake. Quickly. Jump to it.

The MAID *goes out.*

And you. Jump to it. Take police dogs. Search every house. Have them close the frontiers. Have patrol boats comb the seas, even outside our territorial waters. Have powerful searchlights sweep the waves. Make contact with our neighboring states to have her expelled and brought back home. If they invoke the right of asylum or say they haven't signed a treaty of extradition, declare war on them. I want reports every quarter of an hour. And arrest all old women who look as if they might be witches. I want all the caves searched.

The MAID *comes in upstage.*

The four GUESTS, *who were feverishly grabbing swords off the wall and buckling them on and getting tangled up in the process, stop suddenly in the midst of all this activity and turn to face the* MAID.

MAID   Lady Macbett is coming.

LADY DUNCAN *enters.*

She was just on her way up from the cellar, coming up the stairs. (*The* MAID *goes out.*)

> LADY MACBETT, *or rather* LADY DUNCAN, *is rather different from when she last appeared. She is no longer wearing her crown. Her dress is a bit rumpled.*

FIRST *and* SECOND GUESTS (*together*)   Lady Macbett!
THIRD *and* FOURTH GUESTS (*together*)   Lady Macbett!
FOURTH GUEST   Lady Macbett!
MACBETT   You're rather late, madam. I've turned the whole country upside down, looking for you. Where have you been all this time? I'd like an explanation—but not just now. (*To the four* GUESTS) Sit down, gentlemen. Our wedding feast can now begin. Let's eat, drink, and be merry. (*To* LADY MACBETT) Let's forget our little difference. You've come back, my darling, that's the main thing. Let's feast and enjoy ourselves in the company of our dear friends here, who love you as dearly as I do and who have been waiting eagerly for you to arrive.

> *Upstage the projection or the mirrors with the other* GUESTS *and tables appear again.*

FIRST *and* SECOND GUESTS   Long live Lady Macbett!
THIRD *and* FOURTH GUESTS   Long live Lady Macbett!
MACBETT (*to* LADY MACBETT)   Take the place of honor.

FOURTH GUEST   Lady Macbett, our beloved sovereign!

LADY MACBETT *or* LADY DUNCAN   Beloved or not, I am your sovereign. But I'm not Lady Macbett, I'm Lady Duncan—the unhappy but faithful widow of your rightful king, the Archduke Duncan.

MACBETT (*to* LADY DUNCAN)   Are you mad?

Song. Opera.

FIRST GUEST   She is mad.

SECOND GUEST   Is she mad?

THIRD GUEST   She's off her head.

FOURTH GUEST   She's out of her mind.

FIRST GUEST   We were at her wedding!

MACBETT (*to* LADY DUNCAN)   You're my wife. Surely you can't have forgotten. They were all there at the wedding.

LADY DUNCAN   Not my marriage, no. What you saw was Macbett being married to a sorceress who had taken my face, my voice, my body. She threw me in the palace dungeons and chained me up. Just now my chains fell and the bolts drew back as if by magic. I want nothing to do with you, Macbett. I'm not your accomplice. You murdered your master and your friend. Usurper, imposter.

MACBETT   Then how do you know what's been going on?

FIRST GUEST (*singing*)   Yes, how does she know?

SECOND GUEST (*singing*)   She couldn't have known. She was shut up.

THIRD GUEST (*singing*)   She couldn't have known.

GUESTS (*singing*)   She couldn't have known.

LADY DUNCAN (*speaking*)   I heard all about it on the

prison telegraph. My neighbors tapped out the message on the wall in code. I knew everything there was to know. Well, go and look for her—your beautiful wife, the old hag.

MACBETT (*singing*)   Alas, alas, alas! This time it's not a ghost, it's not a ghost this time.

End of Macbett's sung section.

Yes, I'd like to meet that old hag again. She took the way you look and the way you move and made them still more beautiful. She had a more beautiful voice than yours. Where can I find her? She must have disappeared into mist or into thin air. We have no flying machines to track her down, no devices for tracing unidentified flying objects.

GUESTS (*singing together*)   Long live Macbett, down with Macbett. Long live Macbett, down with Macbett! Long live Lady Duncan, down with Lady Duncan! Long live Lady Duncan, down with Lady Duncan!

LADY DUNCAN (*to* MACBETT)   It doesn't look as if your witch is going to help you any more. Unluckily for you, she's abandoned you.

MACBETT   Unluckily? Aren't I lucky to be king of this country? I don't need anyone's help. (*To the* GUESTS) Get out, you slaves.

They go out.

LADY DUNCAN   You won't get off so lightly. You won't be king for long. Macol, Duncan's son, has just come back from Carthage. He has mustered a large and powerful army. The whole country is against you. You've run out of friends, Macbett. (LADY MACBETT *disappears.*)

Shouts of "Down with Macbett! Long live Macol! Down with Macbett! Long live Macol!"

Fanfares. MACOL *enters.*

MACBETT   I fear no one.

MACOL   So I've found you at last. Lowest of the low, despicable, ignoble, abject creature. Monster, villain, scum, murderer. Moral imbecile. Slimy snake. Acrochord. Horned adder. Foul toad. Filthy slob.

MACBETT   Not very impressive. A foolish boy playing at being an avenger. Psychosomatic cripple. Ridiculous imbecile. Heroic puppy. Infatuated idiot. Presumptuous upstart. Greenhorn ninny.

LADY DUNCAN (*to* MACOL, *indicating* MACBETT)   Kill this unclean man, then throw away your tainted sword.

MACBETT   Silly little sod. Shoo! I killed your fool of a father. I wouldn't like to have to kill you, too. It's no good. You can't hurt me. No man of woman born can harm Macbett.

MACOL   They've pulled the wool over your eyes. They were putting you on.

LADY DUNCAN (*to* MACBETT)   Macol isn't my son. Duncan adopted him. Banco was his father, his mother was a gazelle that a witch transformed into a woman. After bringing Macol into the world, she changed back into a gazelle again. I left the court secretly before he was born so that no one would know that I wasn't pregnant. Everyone took him for my son and Duncan's. He wanted an heir, you see.

MACOL I shall resume my father's name and found a dynasty that will last for centuries.

LADY DUNCAN No, Macol. Duncan looked after you. He sent you to Carthage University. You must carry on the family name.

MACBETT Accursed hags. The most cruelly ironic fate since Oedipus.

MACOL I'll kill two birds with one stone—revenge both my natural and adoptive fathers. But I won't give up my name.

LADY DUNCAN Ungrateful boy. You have certain obligations to the memory of Duncan. The whole world is ass-backward. The good behave worse than the bad.

MACOL (*drawing his sword, to* MACBETT) We have some old scores to settle between us. You're not going to draw your stinking breath one moment longer.

MACBETT On your own head be it. You're making a bad mistake. I can only be beaten when the forest marches against me.

> MEN *and* WOMEN *approach* MACBETT *and* MACOL *who are center stage. Each of them is carrying a placard with a tree drawn on it—branches would do as well.*
>
> *Recourse should be had to these two solutions only when there are inadequate technical resources. What should really happen is that the whole set, or at least the upstage part of it, should lumber forward to encircle* MACBETT.

MACOL   Look behind you. The forest is on the march.

MACBETT *turns.*

MACBETT   Shit!

MACOL *stabs* MACBETT *in the back.* MACBETT *falls.*

MACOL   Take away this carrion.

Noises off. Shouts of "Long live Macol! Long live Macol! The tyrant is dead! Long live Macol, our beloved sovereign! Long live Macol!"

And bring me a throne.

Two GUESTS *take up Macbett's body. At the same time the throne is brought on.*

GUEST   Please be seated, my lord.

The other GUESTS *arrive. Some of them put up placards reading "Macol is always right."*

GUESTS   Long live Macol! Long live Banco's dynasty! Long live the king!

Sound of bells. MACOL *is by the throne. The* BISHOP *comes on right.*

MACOL (*to the* BISHOP)   You've come to crown me?
BISHOP   Yes, your Highness.

A poor WOMAN *comes on left.*

WOMAN May your reign be a happy one!

SECOND WOMAN (*coming on right*) Spare a thought for the poor!

MAN (*coming on right*) No more injustice.

SECOND MAN Hate has destroyed our house. Hate has poisoned our souls.

THIRD MAN May your reign usher in a time of peace, harmony and concord.

FIRST WOMAN May your reign be blessed.

SECOND WOMAN A time of joy.

MAN A time of love.

ANOTHER MAN Let us embrace, my brothers.

BISHOP And I will give you my blessing.

MACOL (*standing in front of the throne*) Silence!

FIRST WOMAN He's going to speak.

FIRST MAN The king is going to speak.

SECOND WOMAN Let's listen to what he has to say.

SECOND MAN We're listening, my lord. We'll drink your words.

ANOTHER MAN God bless you.

BISHOP God bless you.

MACOL Quiet, I say. Don't all talk at once. I'm going to make an announcement. Nobody move. Nobody breathe. Now get this into your heads. Our country sank beneath the yoke, each day a new gash was added to her wounds. But I have trod upon the tyrant's head and now wear it on my sword.

A MAN *comes on with Macbett's head on the end of a pike.*

THIRD MAN   You got what was coming to you.

SECOND WOMAN   He got what was coming to him.

FOURTH MAN   I hope God doesn't forgive him.

FIRST WOMAN   Let him be damned eternally.

FIRST MAN   Let him burn in Hell.

SECOND MAN   I hope they torture him.

THIRD MAN   I hope he doesn't get a moment's peace.

FOURTH MAN   I hope he repents in the flames and God refuses him.

FIRST WOMAN   I hope they tear his tongue out and it grows again, and they pull it out again twenty times a day.

SECOND MAN   I hope they roast him on a spit. I hope they impale him. I hope he can see how happy we are. I hope our laughter deafens him.

SECOND WOMAN   I've got my knitting needles. Let's put his eyes out.

MACOL   If you don't shut up at once, I'll set my soldiers and dogs on you.

A forest of guillotines appears upstage as in the First Scene.

MACOL   Now that the tyrant is dead and curses his mother for bringing him into the world, I'll tell you this: My poor country shall have more vices than it had before, more suffer and more sundry ways than ever by me that do succeed.

As Macol's announcement continues, there are murmurs of discontent, amazement and despair from the crowd. At the end of the speech, MACOL is left alone.

In me I know
All the particulars of vice so grafted
That, when they shall be opened, black
Macbett will seem as pure as snow and the
   poor state
Esteem him as a lamb, being compared
With my confineless harms. I grant him bloody.
Luxurious, avaricious, false, deceitful,
Sudden, malicious, smacking of every sin
That has a name: but there's no bottom, none,
In my voluptuousness. Your wives, your daughters,
Your matrons, and your maids, cannot fill up
The cistern of my lust, and my desire
All continent impediments shall o'erbear
That do oppose my will. Better Macbett,
Than such a one to reign. With this there grows
In my most ill-composed affection, such
a staunchless avarice, that now I'm king
I shall cut off the nobles from their lands,
Desire his jewels, and this other's house,
And my more-having will be as a sauce
To make my hunger more, that I shall forge
Quarrels unjust against the good and loyal,
Destroying them for wealth. The king—
   becoming graces
As justice, verity, temp'rance, stableness,
Bounty, perseverance, mercy, lowliness.
Devotion, patience, courage, fortitude,
I have no relish of them, but abound
In the division of each several crime,
Acting it many ways.

The BISHOP, *who was the only one left, goes de-
jectedly out right.*

Now I have power, I shall
Pour the sweet milk of concord into Hell,
Uproar the universal peace, confound
All unity on earth.
First I'll make this Archduchy a kingdom—
and me the king. An empire—and me the
emperor. Super-highness, super-king,
super-majesty, emperor of emperors.

He disappears in the mist.

The mist clears. The BUTTERFLY HUNTER *crosses
the stage.*